THE ALZHEIMER'S

SOURCEBOOK

Frena Gray-Davidson

Balian Books

2012

Arizona

Balian Books
110 Copper St., Bisbee, AZ 85603
email: balianbooks@gmail.com

Cover design and photographs:
Lizann Michaud of Michaud Design

ISBN-13: 978-0615641263

TABLE OF CONTENTS

INTRODUCTION

When I first met Frena Gray-Davidson, she was part of a caregivers group formed to care for an elderly woman in Berkeley, California, in 1986.

Over the years, Frena has utilized her experience as a caregiver as well as her journalistic talent to gather information about how caregiving affects those who receive care, and also how it affects those who give it. She has acquired a great deal of practical knowledge about the business of daily living with a person severely impaired by Alzheimer's disease and has applied her creative insight to the problems inherent in that.

The result is a remarkably innovative and far-reaching approach, which includes a rare sensitivity to the human needs of people with Alzheimer's, along with an acute awareness of the frustrations of people trying to meet those needs.

As a specialist in rehabilitative medicine, I have worked with both adults and children with a range of neurological disabilities. Planning home care for them is often exceedingly difficult.

Families need intensive guidance and support, and very few professionals have devoted the creative energy needed to provide families with a structured approach to coping with caregiving. **The Alzheimer's Sourcebook** opens a gateway for the future of all caregiving.

It describes an approach in which support and care become an organic, constantly adapting process, not a series of actions, but an art and a science of relationship, which grows from needs and issues of the family gathering around its afflicted member.

This book shows how caregiving itself brings growth, a process in which everyone can gain and in which disease is not a villain, but a simple fact to be accommodated and, in the end, transcended as the family pursues a better quality of life for all.

The Alzheimer'sSourcebook offers hope by helping families see caregiving as a journey to be undertaken with intelligence, skill, and caring, not only for the benefit of our loved ones, but for ourselves as well.

Frena once told me that her main intention in this work was to provide light in a dark place. I believe that she has done exactly that.

Janet Lord, M.D.

AUTHOR'S FOREWORD

I became involved with Alzheimer's disease in an entirely accidental way. I had just moved to the United States after more than twelve years of working in Asia as a journalist, when the opportunity arose for me to become part of a caregiving team in Berkeley, California.

I lived in a house with four other amateur caregivers, whose task was to provide homelike care for a 79-year-old woman with Alzheimer's disease.

Until then, I had been completely ignorant of Alzheimer's. When I left England in 1973, no-one was talking about the disease. When I lived in Asia, it was not a topic I ever heard about. I now recognize how blessed I was in knowing nothing.

If I had read all the ugly comments that people routinely make about Alzheimer's disease right to this very day, perhaps I would have been too repelled, scared, or overwhelmed to think of becoming involved with it. My ignorance saved me from being part of that bigotry.

Instead, I learned from Hannah. I learned that even if a person was greatly impaired, she could be fun and loving. Even if she needed a lot of attention, life could be interesting and varied. Even if she never learned my name—and Hannah was never able to remember my name—I always knew that I had a place in her heart. For a year, we made Hannah the center of our lives and our shared purpose was to help her lead as happy and stress-free a life as possible.

Since there were four of us, Hannah had four different lives, plus the remains of her own, and she was a happy woman.

The experience of becoming a caregiver completely transformed my own inner life, and I became deeply involved with the journey that caregivers undertake whenthey become Alzheimer's companions.

Knowing nothing, I learned from people who had Alzheimer's disease. Because I learned from people who have Alzheimer's what the disease is all about, I do not devalue, dismiss, or diminish their experience. I know about the sense of separation, loneliness, and abandonment they feel. I also know they can still enjoy life, and there can be a whole of happiness even after Alzheimer's has begun.

This seems the right place to honor those teachers of mine: Hannah, my first and dearest teacher; Sheila Moon, the poet and psychoanalyst who was able to talk about the profound journey she was undertaking even in the depths of her Alzheimer's disease; Janet, a woman of great humor and character who faced her illness with the courage and determination to live life on her own terms.

Alzheimer's is the great disease of our time. It challenges our fears and exposes the gaps in the cloth of our lives. We are going to have to stop talking about symptoms and begin relating to the people who have this condition.

Only by doing so will we find the answers that keep us from despair and bring light to our own journey. Only by taking the trouble to love will we find that there is something in this ordeal which can actually provide hope and spiritual help.

It is not that Alzheimer's itself has any meaning. Illness just happens to someone, and that someone may be someone you know. The only part of the journey that can contain meaning is our journey to find the answer to the questions: What am I asked to learn? How am I to cope? How must I grow?

In traveling the road, we find answers to those questions, and out of that struggle comes some sense of meaning. This book is intended to be a guide to the journey, a light for the dark places, and a little hope for the times of despair.

You are never alone on this journey. There are millions of us, we caregivers We are to be found in every country and, in the USA, we are to be found in every state, every city, every little town and every little hamlet. There are support groups everywhere, so make sure you go and find those who know your journey well.

Learn from each other, learn from yourself, keep looking for solutions and trust the process of the caregiving journey.

CHAPTER ONE

THE CAREGIVER'S JOURNEY

If you've picked up this book, it's probably because someone you know has Alzheimer's dementia or some other dementia, or you suspect they do. You may be scared—angry, too. You're terrified of the future. You've heard horrible things about Alzheimer's disease. You wonder how you're going to cope. And, deep, inside perhaps you wonder if it could happen to you. You want answers, even though you aren't sure what the questions should be.

This isn't the place to say "don't worry" or "relax." You probably can't do either right now. However, this is the place to say you are not alone. You are on a journey and this book will guide you through many of the more difficult passages. Others have been there before you and have found many different ways to cope. So will you.

Knowledge will give you confidence, and experience will teach you how much you already know. You will have hard days, but you will also have many happy times.

Life is not over because a person has Alzheimer's disease. There will still be adventures, rewards, laughter, and, of course, worry and anger and tears. Let us go together along this pathway you probably never wanted to take and share our time and the wisdom gathered from hundreds of caregivers all over the world. Being a caregiver is a profound spiritual and emotional journey for which most of us are unprepared.

Most of us do not willingly become caregivers. It happens because a disaster overtakes someone we care about or feel responsible for. Looking after a person with Alzheimer's disease is a leap into the maelstrom of caregiving.

You meet all kinds of turbulence, unexpected things happen; you develop skills you did not know you had. It is truly a journey into the unknown.

The caregiver's journey is only slowly becoming familiar to most of us. In all the new awareness brought to us by the psychological self-help movement, the caregiving of others has been the most neglected of all self-explorations. In fact, with the general recognition that unhealthy caring for others has been at the root of many negative family patterns, we have overlooked the importance of developing the skills of healthy caregiving.

Caregiving became unfashionable sometime after mid-20th century, although it was normal in family life in the past. In previous ages, the sick usually stayed at home and certainly died there, ideally surrounded by family members, friends, and neighbors who accompanied them on the last great human journey up to the gates of death itself.

It was the rare human being who never had the experience of caring for another in sickness, and even more rare for a person to have never been present at a death.

These were once essential passages in adjusting to the demands of life, sickness, and death. By contrast, in the 20th century, there was a massive movement away.

Instead, we moved toward placing the sick and dying in hospital care. From the 1940s to the 1990s, the place for the dying was considered to be in a hospital, not at home. This is now changing, largely in response to western medical incapacity to meet the real needs of the dying and their families, or even to acknowledge the reality and inevitability of death. Many people, once again, are opting to die where their life has been most meaningful—at home. This slow return to a previous way of dealing with death and dying comes at a time when many people have become unfamiliar with caregiving.

This book will help you to understand healthy caregiving. It will teach you how to cope and find solutions and how to find meaning and purpose in the caregiving journey, even in the profoundly difficult task of becoming a companion and caregiver to a person with Alzheimer's disease. Even with this dreaded disease, there are rewards to be found in caregiving and there is worth and fulfillment within the struggle.

Right now, of course, you just want to know more about Alzheimer's disease and the other dementias and get some ideas on coping with it. You want a few key facts that will magically enable you to become an effective caregiver and take away the problems of your daily life.

However, you will soon find out − if you have not already − that just learning facts about this particular disease is not enough.

You probably already know that your doctor and your social worker and your neurologist may not help you find the answers to daily life caregiving problems.

Only the collective experience of many caregivers can do that. That is the knowledge and understanding that this book offers you on your journey. This book has been written by one caregiver with over 20 years of living and working with Alzheimer's disease and other dementias. As a support group facilitator and a workshop presenter, I have also distilled the experiences of hundreds of other caregivers. I have additionally been educated by the errors that I have made.

I will share with you what we all have learned from our encounters with dementia. Even this is not the end of your exploration. It is true that finding approaches to solving problems is essential if you are to have any peace in your daily life. However, there is something more that will make your task meaningful and help you overcome the despair that weighs down so many Alzheimer caregivers.

To meet this challenge successfully, you need to explore the profound meaning of this journey. That meaning is contained in the question: how am I asked to grow? And, as caregivers, we are asked to grow in how we choose to do the journey of caregiving. We might find deep meaning the disease itself, or not. That is not necessary. The meaning is largely in how we grow, how we adapt, how we care for ourselves in the journey of caring for someone else. How we choose to live our life.

Without considering all these issues, you may succumb to the debilitating anger and depression that weighs down the people who regard this only as a cruel and meaningless affliction.

This is not to say that anyone recommends dementia caregiving as guaranteed to be a rewarding undertaking. However, you cannot face the journey day after day if you get locked into despair or hopelessness that consumes your energy.

You will miss the small pleasures and delights that can come when you spend time in the Alice-in-Wonderland world of someone with dementia. You will miss the areas in which an afflicted person can actually grow despite the illness. Noticing that growth and appreciating it helps reduce stress for you, as the caregiver, as well as for the person with Alzheimer's.

It helps you focus on what is positive and allows you to show appreciation for who that person is now, instead of being locked into mourning who that person used to be. Because that public myth that people with dementia are empty, lost and gone-away is just that, a myth. There is plenty of person still there, waiting and hoping that you might notice. Bad attitudes from others are what cause much of the emotional attrition of this disease.

It is the constant message that all is lost—that this disease is cruel and demeaning, that essentially it cannot be coped with—which overwhelms caregivers.

This book has been written to help you understand what the deeper elements of this disease mean to us as human beings, what growth is possible, and what personal development and spiritual strength come from bringing all your compassion, creativity, sense of humor, and ability to each day of living with Alzheimer's disease.

The Chinese say, when you cannot change a situation, then you have to change your mind. This book will help you to see that even the hardest situations give us some choices about how we deal with them.

Right now, the dementia situation cannot be changed, though we can hope the future will be different, as medical science tackles the complexities of this disease and unravels its secrets. Right now, you may have to learn to live with it.

To do that, you may have to make some significant changes in your life. Since so much of what you read and hear about Alzheimer's disease is negative, here are some positive items of information you may not know:

• Many people with Alzheimer's disease become much more open emotionally, showing affection and love as they never did before.

• The human journey to inward peace and resolution still continues for the person with Alzheimer's disease, and achieving happiness is entirely possible.

• As a caregiver, you can become a valuable part of that journey, both in helping the person you care for and in pursuing your own pathway. You grow heart and soul.

• Many people with totally fragmented short-term memory function have astonishingly accurate long-term memory.

Therefore, Alzheimer's disease does not preclude the final coming to terms with the primary relationships in life that is a normal part of the aging process for many older people. Even people who are seriously impaired with dementia are often still clearly involved with this process of trying to find resolution. This is why they will see their mothers and fathers or why they sometimes wait for their parents to visit them.

All human beings are somewhat in thrall to the shadow of their parents, alive or dead. The death of parents does not, by any means, release the child from patterns of need and reaction. Memory problems often cause people with Alzheimer's disease to forget that their parents are dead, but for them, as for the rest of us, parents are never truly dead. Therefore, the issue of finding peace can be very much a part of Alzheimer's disease.

Sometimes, persons with Alzheimer's repeat stories of long-ago traumas and heartbreaks again and again. This is to bring resolution to unhappy or frightening memories. Once you understand this as a caregiver, you can help the person you look after to reach a state of acceptance and letting go of the past. It will also help you to see that this is part of the meaning of this difficult passage in life. It gives an emotional space within the person for real things to happen.

This is one aspect of the journey that has been unexplored in the literature on the disease. In fact, persons with Alzheimer's disease and their caregivers have suffered a great deal from the silences regarding the areas of hope and growth that surround them. We need to know about these positive aspects so that we can appreciate and encourage them.

• People with Alzheimer's also often keep certain special abilities they had—singers still sing, musicians still play, the spiritual will still be spiritually awake, although they will need more feeling and less intellectual ambiance for their spirituality;

• Pleasures are still pleasures—good food, enjoying pets, appreciating love.

• The sense of humor remains;

• The awareness of sexuality—even the ability to flirt—often remains.

The purpose of reminding you about all this is that often we are so caught up in what people can no longer do that we forget to acknowledge and enjoy what they can do. Some persons with Alzheimer's actually develop new ways to be creative, which is a true triumph of the human spirit. People who have never painted before can be led into painting with the right teacher. Group poetry-making can be a successful and moving venture. Music is a powerful communication tool that still speaks clearly to the impaired. In the emotional range, many dementia-impaired people become more openly loving, more accepting of love, and more appreciative of tenderness and care.

Emotional capacity becomes more naked in those who no longer have the mind structure to create barriers to hide their feelings. In many ways, the deepest revelation of the Alzheimer journey was revealed to me by Sheila Moon, a great Jungian analyst with dementia. She taught me that it is a kind of passage from the mind into the heart.

For the caregiver, one of the great teachings of this journey is that it reveals to us that a person is still fully a person, even when impaired in memory and mental function. It demonstrates daily that love is always important.

Love, in fact, will be the greatest basis of all your management skills. For some of you, this idea will be a relief, because you already know you love the person you care for. If you feel despair or a sense of doom because you have troubled or unresolved feelings toward the person—for example, your mother was a lousy mother but now needs you to act as her good mother—don't give up.

This book will help you unravel some of those tangles too. Resolution and forgiveness are possible for everyone willing to do the personal work needed. For other caregivers, such as spouses of people with Alzheimer's, personal growth and resolution come with accepting a change of role and forgiveness of the losses caused by this disease.

Once we learn to accept things as they are in the present moment—and we can learn to do that—everything else becomes possible.

These are the issues of the caregiver's journey. In our society today, we often value people for what they do or have and usually much less for what they are. If we judge people to be damaged in any way, especially damaged in mind, we attach even less value to them. It is very hard for us to accept that every person is a valuable person and that every person has a deep and abiding need to be loved. Unfortunately, we tend to treat the impaired as less of a person and therefore as less lovable.

We also treat him or her as less deserving of being treated as a whole person and as less needing of such treatment. Commonly, we hear people say that the person with Alzheimer's disease becomes like a child, and often the people around them treat them that way. However, no-one who is past the age of eleven is a child. An 80-year-old woman with severe dementia is an 80-year-old woman with all the experiences, dreams, hopes, and disappointments that go with long life.

She may need us to communicate with her at the primary functioning level of a small child, but she also needs, and has a right to be respected as an adult. The good caregiver will do both. By using your understanding, you will learn to see the person as she or he really is.

People do not become simpler with Alzheimer's disease. They become more complex, and we need a complexity of skills to relate to them. Relationship is the center of the caregiver's journey. The average person with Alzheimer's usually does not need much nursing, or indeed may not need any. The unrelenting need is for companionship, understanding, compassion, supervision - oh yes, and love.

You probably understand by now why the path of the care-giver is a spiritual journey. This journey asks of us that we accept another person as always whole in spirit, as needing our unconditional love, and as being valued here and now as the person he or she is.

When we only hark back to who this person used to be, we cause anguish for ourselves and create continuing anguish for the person with Alzheimer's disease. Many special moments are available in the here and now if we let go of the person we wish someone to be.

In the case of a caregiver who is a family member, this means letting go of mother in the role of mother or husband in the role of spouse. This is hard and painful to do, but if we cannot do it, we create more pain every minute of our day.

We also do better if we forgive the person, and the list of items up for forgiveness may well be extensive. We must:

• Forgive the illness and its symptoms;
• Forgive any wrongs that person did to us in the past;
• Forgive for never being able to have things "right" again;
• Forgive for the plans we made that have been spoiled;
• Forgive the forgetting;
• Forgive that person whose illness constantly reminds us how we fail as caregivers;
• Forgive ourselves for the ways we fail as caregivers.

What is good about this journey for the caregiver? It teaches us many of the deepest spiritual truths in everyday life.

No sitting alone in a forest clearing for the Alzheimer caregiver. No, it is unremitting daily life experience that brings the caregiver to the exact same place that the forest meditator eventually hopes to come to—the place of unconditional love. There is nothing ethereal, otherworldly, or wishy-washy about this love. Unconditional love does not mean perfect behavior, nor is it sentimental. It is basic, real, connected, and ordinary—that is what makes it extraordinary, of course.

You will receive constant cueing about how you are relating to the person you look after. In Alzheimer's, there can be confusion and bewilderment on both the part of the caregiver and the person with the condition. Nevertheless, certain things will always be very clear.

The person you look after will become your teacher in those things. When you are angry, even if you hide it from yourself, your anger may well be reflected back by the person with Alzheimer's. When you are anxious, hurried, or brusque, that person may respond with loss of function, bizarre behavior, or confusion, and uncertainty.

You are accountable for everything you feel, because it brings a response. You will get to know yourself probably better than you wanted to. The enormous plus in all this is that you can be exactly who you are with the person who has Alzheimer's. You will always be accepted as you are because memory loss removes expectation and the ability to recollect your failings. You can be silly or emotional or irritable and you will always be forgiven because it will always be forgotten. This is a giant spiritual gift because, through another person's forgetting, you will forgive yourself. You get to start afresh all the time with a person who has Alzheimer's disease. Each day is a new beginning. You can regard that as a curse or as a blessing. If you are wise, you will work with it as a blessing.

You will discover the power of love each moment because it is the best practical way to make life work with Alzheimer's. A mistake? You give a hug. Fear? You give a hug. Anxiety? You give a back rub. Restlessness?

20

Make a joke and give a hug. Love will become your most reliable management technique. If this begins to sound as if you have to do all the giving, certainly there is an element of truth to that. However, if you continue to learn to be a good caregiver, you will also learn to receive.

Get a hug, get a back rub, share some of your sadness. The person with Alzheimer's is perfectly capable of giving and sharing. You do not have to always stand alone. Although it is true that the disease causes great losses that probably make you feel sad and sometimes very lonely, still there are many times you could share being together. These might not be in the ways you want, but that is where you just have to accept what is.

Usually you can find ways to be less alone. You can be completely honest. You can say that you feel angry or frustrated or lonely and it will not be held against you. Honesty works well in Alzheimer's. In fact, it is the best possible policy. Later chapters will show you how to communicate well and how to understand what is being communicated to you, but meanwhile know that honesty works as one of your best tools.

Perhaps the deepest spiritual lesson in all of this is that unless we tend to our own needs we cannot tend to another's. Caregivers who do not look after themselves often become inadequate caregivers because they have exhausted their inner resources. We must ask so that we can receive. One person alone cannot deal with Alzheimer's. It is false pride to think so. It is not even fair to try since it will mean poor caregiving and even lead to abuse of the person who is sick. We have to ask others for help, and in that way we open pathways for others to show love.

Often, outsiders can be more loving and accepting than family caregivers can, because the outsider does not have the psychic history that the family carries.

The caregiver who rejects help from others, who insists on standing alone, who wants to control the whole situation, only comes to exhaustion and despair. This is the typical over-achieving caregiver who fills Alzheimer literature, and is the most commonly seen figure in Alzheimer stories in the media.

Up to now, society has stood back to watch this overachiever with respect and awe, assuming this must be the true picture of Alzheimer care. However, this image does not serve anyone well. It is time to stop applauding over-achieving in caregiving because it leads to bad caregiving and destroys both giver and receiver. Many of the so-called problem behaviors of Alzheimer's come from situations where the over-achieving caregivers are trying to maintain control.

This is not to criticize, but just to gently indicate that it is time to let go of that damaging stereotype and work toward real health in caregiving, just as we are seeking health in other dependent relationships in our society. There is nothing noble about a person who becomes ill from caregiving.

It is a tragic waste of human effort and caring. This book will teach you how to avoid the traps of becoming an over-achieving caregiver and help you to plan your outreach for help.

Caregiving teaches us, finally, that human beings need love all the way to the gates of death and that love always matters. Often families fade out of the scene once someone is in full-time care. They say, "She doesn't even know me," when the issue is not knowing but loving. Someone who cannot intellectually get your name right still needs love.

Moreover, if we really try to understand Alzheimer's, then we come to realize that when your mother calls you "Mother," it is not that she has forgotten your role as her daughter, it is that she needs your maternal love in her sickness, and does, in fact, recognize you as deeply important. If we can take the risk of feeling our pain, and our loss, then we can be free to love as much as is needed—that is, unconditionally.

If we can face the terror of the disease, then we can be free to love instead of running away. When we can go to the nursing home to see Grandma, and hold her hand even if she cannot acknowledge our ego needs, then we are demonstrating exactly what family is supposed to be about. After all, if the family does not supply Grandma's need for love, who exactly is supposed to be there fulfilling that need?

When we give our full accepting love in the here-and-now moment, we find the average person with Alzheimer's can experience a lot of happiness in an average day. Alzheimer's strikes at the roots of our terror of depending upon others, and not getting enough love.

This is not on the whole a physically painful disease. The most emotionally difficult stages for people with the disease are usually the early stages. Later on, with the right caregivers around, daily life can be very pleasant. Many people in the later stages enter a kind of blissfulness in which it is obvious that they have reached emotional resolution.

While there may be times when the person becomes agitated, this usually does not last long. It passes, and is not remembered. People with Alzheimer's do not hold on to what distresses or frightens them in the moment. The blessing of the disease is the same as the curse— forgetfulness.

The real anguish of this disease is carried by family members and also by those who have never been around it. This anguish is caused by the psychic input from the world that says this is surely the most terrible disease there is. That attitude comes mainly from those who do not understand the disease and from those caregivers who do not take care of themselves and therefore become depressed, dysfunctional, and despairing.

Much of that is a by-product of lack of sleep and overwhelming feelings. Perhaps we need not dread Alzheimer's so much if we know that it causes little physical pain and that its emotional pain can often be greatly alleviated by good caregiving. If we do not feel the disease is demeaning, the sufferer is freed from feeling demeaned. So it helps if we let go of some of our own judgments about this illness.

The bright side for you as the caregiver is that, even if you never wanted to be a caregiver, you can learn to do it well, and you will reap all the spiritual and emotional benefits. You may also incur all the immense emotional costs too, so be sure to read all the chapters in this book that will help you with details and problems.

If you dislike the word "spiritual", ignore it, and just do the job well anyway. You will still get many benefits. If you think it is insulting to have to read about love when you want to read only the latest information on Alzheimer treatment, that's okay.

Read these chapters, get on with caregiving, and check in again in a few weeks' time to see if love is any part of your agenda yet. It may not matter to anyone else if you do not deal with the issues of love in your life, but it will matter to the person with Alzheimer's disease, and that person will let you know about it in a thousand subtle and not so subtle ways.

If you are a caregiver or about to become one, congratulations! You are joining a little band of warriors who are not deeply appreciated in this world where examinations, technology, and documentation have taken over the world of caregiving but have left many people who need loving care bereft and alone. The home caregiver is one of the great unsung heroes of today.

If you are one, know that there are many others like you. You will find them at support group meetings all over the country—brave people living the ordinary life in extraordinary ways.

You have chosen, or have had thrust upon you, one of the great human journeys. As an Alzheimer companion, you have elected to accompany another human being into one of the most mysterious pathways of the human spirit. You will be the light for someone else's darkness. You will have to walk through what is still a scarcely known underworld, the shadow side of memory.

This book will help you enormously on that journey with all the facts and practical information, and how-to techniques, but you already have the only real weapon needed against the shadows.

The name of that weapon is Love.

CHAPTER TWO

BEFORE DIAGNOSIS

"Looking back, I can see now that Dad's illness started years before we knew. He stopped going out to play cards with his buddies. He always used to go every Friday night, but gradually he began not bothering. I asked him why and he said he just didn't want to, but I suppose it was because he couldn't manage the game any more and didn't want to say so. It was his secret. Over the next few years, he let more and more of his old life go. He even stopped driving. He said he couldn't see any more, but I think that was just his excuse," says Ken, whose father is seventy-five and has Alzheimer's disease.

Many times, long before a person is actually diagnosed as having Alzheimer's disease, there are small indicators of something wrong. These signs often puzzle or alarm family members, but until they have accumulated sufficiently to cause major disquiet, their real significance is not really understood. Only in looking back are they seen as signposts of Alzheimer's.

As one family member put it, "Mom was always a bit strange, to be honest. She had her odd ways which we kids all just thought of as being Mom's personal style. For example, one thing she did was to dry paper towels over a toaster. She did it for years and we didn't really even know it was strange at the time. We just knew this was what Mom did.

"Of course, now that she's been diagnosed with Alzheimer's, we often ask ourselves if this was a very early sign and no one knew it."

Since dementia takes many forms, it is hard to list all the questionable behaviors that may indicate its presence. Even if we could list them all, we could not be sure what they signified.

"We thought Grandma was just upset after Grandpa died. She wouldn't go out. She didn't have her hair done any more. We always used to have big Sunday lunches at Grandma's house and she did all the cooking, but then she said she couldn't be bothered any more. Then bailiffs came from the sheriff's office and Dad found she hadn't paid any property taxes for years. He found all the bills in a drawer. She nearly lost the house," says Adam, whose grandmother was diagnosed at sixty-nine with Alzheimer's disease.

A whole range of odd behaviors make up each person's idiosyncratic style. If we later develop Alzheimer's, our own families will not know whether to attribute these idiosyncrasies to our disease or to our personal styles of being. Most Alzheimer indicators are behaviors that accumulate until they actually interfere with normal life. Until they do interfere with a person's functioning, we cannot claim them as indicators of Alzheimer's disease. In fact, it is important that we do not. It will become clear as you read on that the so-called Alzheimer symptoms can be signs of many other conditions.

Some may be caused by medications (the average older person is taking at least six medications at any one time). Therefore, be alert to possible warning signs but do not make any assumptions. Experts in the Alzheimer field warn us that many older people with various problems are categorized as having Alzheimer's disease when in fact they do not. This particular dementia has become a catch-all basket into which all kinds of cases are thrown, including conditions that could well be treated. Residing in every Alzheimer's care unit are people suspected by the staff of not having Alzheimer's at all and who have never been formally diagnosed.

Even the medical profession makes this mistake, so it is obvious that amateur Alzheimer spotters only confuse things further. No amateur can accurately classify a symptom. Even medical experts can do so only with extensive testing. In fact, the final diagnosis of Alzheimer's disease is made only after all other possibilities have been eliminated. It is a diagnosis that basically says, "We can't find anything else that fits, so we can reasonably assume that what we are left with must be Alzheimer's disease."

The diagnosis is usually stated to be "a dementia of the Alzheimer's type," sometimes shortened to DAT.

If someone you know exhibits a number of the signs and symptoms discussed below, proper medical investigation is needed. These signs are warnings that something is wrong, whether that something is depression or liver trouble or Alzheimer's disease.

Also be aware that every individual with Alzheimer's has a personal style of presenting the disease. These variations cause confusion and questions among family members. Alzheimer's sufferers have certain universal problems, the most obvious being memory loss, but other symptoms vary widely, so much so that some medical experts are currently suggesting that there are several different kinds of Alzheimer's disease. Some think that this is not so much a specific disease as a collection of identifying behaviors and variable symptoms—in other words, a syndrome.

If you are worried about a family member who presents a number of these symptoms, encourage the person to get a complete checkup, including neurological testing, CAT scans, and laboratory tests. Beforehand, speak privately to the doctor about your concerns so that the doctor will include a memory test while interviewing the patient and will be alert to possible cover-up of problems by the patient.

It is typical for Alzheimer patients to deny there is anything wrong with them, often in a confident and convincing manner. Many family members report their frustration over this.

"I told the doctor my husband was having severe memory problems, but the doctor just asked him if he ever forgot anything and my husband said cheerfully, 'Oh no, in fact I've got a great memory.' Frankly, I could have killed the pair of them!" reports one frustrated wife. It was a year later before her husband was finally diagnosed.

That was only after she had insisted on a full Alzheimer's workup from a neurologist. Some families have communication problems with their doctors over their early suspicions. Some physicians shrug off the concerns by vague phrases like, "What can you expect at his age?" or "There may be a little senility there."

There are many good doctors and it is essential to have one when dealing with Alzheimer's, even if this means changing your doctor. Since Alzheimer's is so variable, you need an experienced doctor to deal with it.

Those who work with many Alzheimer sufferers and talk with their families recognize that there is a much earlier phase than the one normally identified as "early stage." This is what I have named the "invisible phase." It covers the period of time—that could extend for many years—in which only the individual concerned knows or suspect there is something wrong. One woman, diagnosed at seventy-four, had written in her diaries twenty years before that she was experiencing problems with her thinking. She had what she called "these terrible absentmindednesses of mine," that involved both memory lapses and problems in thinking things through.

Another woman, a Jungian psychologist, noted a series of dreams she had 30 years before being diagnosed with Alzheimer's disease in which doctors told her she had an incurable brain disease. She did not interpret these dreams literally and it was only her later illness that retrospectively suggested that she should have.

Many anecdotes like this suggest interesting questions about how some people have a deep inner knowledge of their true state of health, even before any visible signs of illness are present. The invisible phase, during which the individual lives privately with the growing awareness that something is wrong, is seen by others only in behavior changes, often inexplicable at the time. An outgoing, gregarious man gave up his social life entirely, telling his wife he just could not be bothered. At the time, she put it down to the demands of his work, but later she saw it as the beginning of Alzheimer's disease.

Another woman stopped playing mahjong with her friends. When her son asked her why, she answered vaguely, "Oh, I don't like those people any more." Other people show no outward signs that they are troubled and yet later discoveries reveal that they were aware of their encroaching illness. One woman started collecting articles on memory loss dating from her early forties, even though she worked at a demanding job until normal retirement age and was not actually diagnosed until she was eighty. Her family discovered her secret cache of cuttings after she went into skilled nursing care.

A man who never drank to excess began to drink heavily and to throw temper tantrums at home for a period of several years, during which his wife was frantic. "I thought Bill hated me. I thought he was going to leave me. He used to scream at me and throw his dinner plate against the walls. I had no idea what was going on at that time."   When Bill was finally identified as having Alzheimer's disease, his wife understood that he had been reacting in sheer terror to his knowledge that he was losing control within. Either because of denial or simply because he did not know the nature of what was going on, Bill never spoke about his fears to his wife. When he was finally diagnosed and the doctor broke the news to he and his wife together, Bill said, "Thank God! Oh, thank God! I thought I was going crazy!"

This is not an uncommon reaction among Alzheimer sufferers. While their families are afraid to mention the word Alzheimer's to them,   they themselves are often convinced that they are going mad or becoming stupid. They cannot talk about their unformulated fears and feelings. Instead, they act them out. All of these signs could indicate problems with thought processes and the gradual failure of rational thinking ability, together with emotional intensity.

Often family members notice changes but cannot identify what they signify, either because they really do not know or because they are in denial. It is hard for families to admit that something is wrong. For a long time, individual members just harbor their secret suspicions.

"My mother started avoiding people, even family members," says Mary, whose 85-year-old mother lives in an Alzheimer care unit. "Once, her sister came to visit and my mother refused even to come out of her room the whole time her sister was there. Yet they'd always been close. It was really embarrassing and I didn't understand it at all.

Maybe she didn't want anyone to know there was something wrong with her and she thought her sister would realize."

Often, the only sign of trouble is a mood change—depression, anxiety, or increasing dependence even over very small things. These lead to greater emotional stress for both family members and for the person who is finally manifesting the first visible signs of disease. One woman of seventy-four was told by her youngest son to become more independent at a time when, unknown to him, she was reminding herself who her own children were by writing memos in her diary: "My youngest son is Myron and he teaches high school students. My oldest son is Dieter and he's a doctor in Chicago." Her sudden extra dependency came out of her knowledge that she was losing her memory.

Another family identified their mother's early dementia as "Mother's nerves" and explained her tears and tantrums as a sign that she and their father were not enjoying their retirement. As true as that observation was, it was far from being the real story. They tried to deal with their mother's growing incapacity by bringing in household help, except that their mother would fire the help behind their backs. She was not ready to reveal her neediness other than to family members, who in turn were not ready to acknowledge it.

Thus, although the common medical term for the cumulative gathering of visible symptoms is early stage Alzheimer's, we can now see that this is not necessarily a correct description of how far the disease has progressed. Family members must not think this term literally means the disease is in its beginnings.

After the invisible stage comes the "visible early stage." During this time, which again may extend for many years or a few months, the family sees a number of disquieting signs. This list could be endless, since any kind of variation might appear in any individual. Basically, these signs all add up to decreasing competency in daily life, increasing memory problems, and signs of emotional distress. Obviously, there are many possible reasons for these developments, which is why it is important to persuade the person to seek help.

This can be the hardest thing of all, since most families tend to respect the desire of members to remain independent as long as possible. They do not want to interfere. However, in general, families intervene too late rather than too soon. It is almost unknown for a family to intervene inappropriately early. Be confident that by the time you have noticed signs of distress accumulating, you are dealing with an important problem. Even when the whole family recognizes there is a problem, they often hesitate to interfere until the disease becomes much more advanced. If this is your case, it would be a good idea for all your family members to talk together.

You all want to agree on how to ensure life quality, tactful help, and discreet monitoring of the impaired person's lifestyle. Consider a shopping plan, a visiting plan, a meal schedule, help with household papers and bills, and so on. It is not a kindness to leave people with dementia to cope beyond their capacity to do so. It places a heavy burden on them and undoubtedly adds to their stress tremendously. Demented people cannot run their own lives. It is that simple.

Of course, it is hard to know exactly how to intervene. Most people resent your butting in. Whatever their degree of stress, your own family members hardly ever say, "Why, yes, thank you for suggesting I can't run my own life. I'm so grateful you want to take it over for me!"

Family members need to get together to discuss what they are seeing. Ideally, everyone makes an input into this discussion and it becomes a reality check for the whole family. This is important since the early visible stages of Alzheimer's are often somewhat nebulous—a fading of capacity rather than a clearly delineated set of circumstances. It is helpful for everyone to make a list of the problems. Write down each incident or symptom and discuss whether this adds up to illness. Normal idiosyncrasies should be left off the list. For example, if Mother has always had unkempt hair, then this should not be listed. You are looking for changes that indicate a decline is going on, a growing inability to manage life as before.

When only one or two indicators are found, assume that this slight decline is within the range of normal aging and stop worrying. If the list is long, obviously there are problems. It is normal for people approaching their final years to show a certain amount of withdrawal from the things of everyday life. In our new awareness of Alzheimer's, we must not label all such withdrawals as dementia. A woman of ninety who begins to forget names and addresses from the present when she is inwardly concentrating upon setting her primary relationships to peace before death does not deserve the label of Alzheimer's disease.

Even if you have compiled a symptom list applying to your family member, this is not necessarily a reason to rush the ailing person into medical or nursing care. Increasing family support could help to keep the person coping with limited independence. Family members could take over certain household tasks and see whether the situation gets better, worse, or is holding at a plateau. Unless an actual trauma of some kind occurs, family members need not hurry into life-changing decisions.

When trauma occurs, however, rapid decline results. Almost every family story of Alzheimer's disease mentions that the major signs of decline come on quickly after trauma. People manage more or less for a long time, even with an accumulation of problems; then comes a sudden catastrophe. After that, seemingly, they become overwhelmed.

Some researchers suggest that this may come about through a collapse of the immune system as a result of trauma. Autopsy research has shown that the actual physical deterioration of the brain bears no relationship to the outward signs of dementia. A number of people, autopsied for other causes of death, have been found to have all the signs of severe Alzheimer's-like brain deterioration and yet showed no dementia behaviors. This suggests that the physical attack on the brain is not always the main factor in deterioration. The other factor lies in the mystery of human resistance to disease. When that collapses through stress, it is as if the disease suddenly runs on apace. This probably accounts for the family stories that say, "Mother was fine until Dad died. Then she suddenly got Alzheimer's disease."

The kinds of trauma that may lead to increased manifestations of possible Alzheimer's disease include the following:

- The death of a spouse, close family member, or good friend;
- A change of residence;
- A car accident, even with no injuries;
- A fall, whether with injury or not;
- Surgery, especially under general anesthesia;
- Being the victim of threatened or actual violence, such as being mugged;
- Being the victim of a burglary;
- Retirement or the unwelcome loss of a job;
- Developing another serious illness;
- Emotional stress;
- General failure to thrive, a term used normally only for infants and small children but equally applicable to older people undergoing adverse age changes or emotional reactions.

There are a few physical indicators of possible Alzheimer's disease. These may include the sudden development of intense sugar cravings, even in people who never liked sweet things before, and the loss of the sense of smell. We do not yet understand these factors, although we can make guesses. Dietary researchers assert that the average person with Alzheimer's disease uses up some 4,000 calories per day, enough for heavy physical labor. This burning of calories, which may be due to the whole physical system being in overdrive merely to cope, probably accounts for the sugar cravings that are universal in dementia sufferers.

Other early signs are not in the person but in the environment, small clues that something is wrong. "I kept finding sheets in the oven and when I asked Mom why they were there, she'd say she was drying them. That was the only thing, and after a while it even seemed fairly normal to me. I just thought, 'Oh yes, there's Mom's sheets in the oven again.' She didn't have it switched on, so there wasn't any danger," Mary recalls.

Finding things in strange places—matches in the freezer, clothes in the oven—indicates a shift in thought processes. Hearing stories that just do not add up or make sense. Finding your family member cannot account for a day's activities at all. Unusual discrepancies in management of household finances, such as paying a bill several times, or not at all—all these indicate severe problems. Then there is the refrigerator test—the refrigerator of the average Alzheimer's patient contains one dried lemon, two eggs, several ancient containers of food from restaurants, and two gallons of chocolate ice cream.

These are only signs of distress if they represent a change in behavior and life management. If a woman has always hoarded food items, then twenty cans of corn in her pantry do not necessarily represent Alzheimer's. The typical Alzheimer refrigerator could also be the typical young student's refrigerator, so the key again is whether a change has appeared. Likewise, gradual decline in cleanliness of a house, management of a garden, or cooking ability may be signs that something is wrong.

If you are a family member worried about someone and you find that much of this chapter applies, what do you do? If your relative admits the problem, that is one thing. If your relative refuses even to admit there is anything wrong, you have a serious dilemma. You may have to stand by for years before crisis offers a chance for intervention.

Rather than worry about your frustration or fears, concentrate on what you can do. You can help where it is acceptable—spring cleaning, taking the person out for a meal, shopping. You can also join a support group. Many people who attend Alzheimer support groups are there because they suspect someone has dementia, not because they know.

Go to see your relative's doctor to express your worries. This will enable the doctor to be aware of possible memory and dementia issues when next examining your relative. That, for the time being, is all you can do. Often, being a good friend to someone with Alzheimer's simply consists of acceptance, support, and love, with practical aid whenever it can be given and accepted. Try not to project your fears about Alzheimer's on the person you suspect may have it. Instead, just be open to finding ways to be in that person's life that help both of you relate to each other. Someone who fears he or she has something wrong is much more likely to confide those fears in a trusted and loved friend or relative and especially if that person does not harangue, demean and scold in the anxiety of worrying about someone else.

So be prepared, if you know someone who shows a number of the signs mentioned in this chapter, to serve by standing and waiting.

CHAPTER THREE

ALZHEIMER'S DISEASE

Wisdom is the principal thing; therefore get wisdom: and with all thy getting, get understanding. Proverbs 4:7

This chapter contains a picture of the typical course of Alzheimer's disease, what is currently known about it, recent research, current uses of medication, and possible medical developments in the future. It is very important to remember, however, that everyone does Alzheimer's disease in a totally individual way. Certain symptoms may be universal—memory problems, for example—but otherwise there can be great variation from person to person and even in one person from day to day.

Never assume that the typical course of the disease outlined here is what will happen to your parent. In fact, very few people reach the so-called last stages of Alzheimer's disease. Although that is the picture most people imagine and dread on behalf of their own family member, only about one person in 40 actually becomes helpless and fetal. In reality, that is rare.

Dementia is not a new disease, only the name is new. Back in 500 B.C. Solon, the famous Greek lawyer and philosopher, wrote that impaired judgment from old age could cause a will to be invalid.

It is only our current awareness that is new. One of the possible reasons why we hear so much about Alzheimer's disease now is because of the huge increase in the number of people living longer. While the actual span of human life has not really extended, the percentage of people living to its extent has mega-jumped. So, what we are now seeing is an aging process apparent in very many elders. Although current concentration on Alzheimer's disease is frightening for some people, it actually has positive aspects. We now know, for example, that people in old age can reasonably expect good health. After all, if 10 percent of people aged 65 have Alzheimer's, that means 90 out of every 100 do not. That is a pretty good set of figures. Alzheimer's disease is perhaps the best-known, most-feared disease of this century by older people. It is an organic brain disease of unknown origin. Alzheimer's is not a mental illness, but a physical deterioration of the brain which disrupts normal brain processes. It sets up physical roadblocks throughout the entire brain, damaging the message system which controls everyday functions and mental organization. Essentially, Alzheimer's causes the computer of the brain to malfunction, bringing life into disarray..

The overall picture of dementia – which includes Alzheimer's Disease, since it is also a dementia – is listed in the American Psychiatric Association's diagnostic manual, the D.S.M. IV.

The Association states that dementia has an insidious onset, with a gradual progressive course. All other specific possible causes are excluded through the complete and extensive Alzheimer's work-up which details a person's history with physical examination, and laboratory tests. After findings no other traceable causes to account for the presence of dementia, a diagnosis is then made.

From then on, a typical picture of what to expect involves a multifaceted loss of intellectual abilities, such as memory, judgment, abstract thought, and other higher cortical functions. Probable changes in personality and behavior may be seen. Normal brain function is disrupted and slowly erodes further. The course of the disease has three stages: early (or first) stage, middle (or second) stage, and final (or third, last, or terminal) stage.

Although some accounts include up to nine stages, that is really a device to explain Alzheimer's to non-medical people, especially family members. It is not a medically-based explanation, more a social explanation so that families can more easily   understand the disease progression.

From my own observations, I would add that there is also an initial "invisible" stage, which is apparent only to the sufferer, inwardly aware of frightening changes in memory and thinking processes. While some people may share this with family or friends, most keep very quiet about it.

In the early visible stage of the disease, a person typically has signs of memory loss—forgetting names, events, day, and year—and may show some decline in intellectual ability, unable to learn new skills or procedures or to carry out abstract tasks. If the person is still working, problems at work may appear, with a drop in performance or sudden early retirement. Some signs of personality change may begin—increased withdrawal, less enjoyment of daily pleasures, dropping previous routines—but these are likely to be subtle.

These difficulties increase as the person proceeds from early to middle stage, typically from two to ten years after diagnosis. Typical of the second stage is the appearance of much more apparent memory problems—forgetting names of neighbors, family members, and daily events. There may be an inability to understand what is going on, less ability to express things, lack of grooming, failure to keep up household routines, not paying bills, and an inability to manage money. It will be harder for the person in the middle stage to follow explanations and arguments, and this may look like stubbornness, but it is not. Activities may be dropped altogether, without explanation, plus reading and writing problems, changes in physical posture and movement, and refusing to go out. Apparently-irrational fears may develop: "The neighbors are stealing from me." Accidents keep happening—car accidents unaccounted for or blamed on others, pots left burning, appliances left on.

Personality changes may occur: outbursts of anger, hostility, weeping, anxiety attacks, depression. Much more noticeable signs will appear, and family members will probably become aware at this point, if not before, of a serious problem. In fact, this is when family intervention begins. However, there are no clearly delineated differences between the early and middle stages because the individual pathway varies so much. Often, you may want to know for sure at what stage your parent is but receive an inaccurate answer from medical professionals. That's because there is no objective answer. To an extent, each person does dementia in his or her own way. Most of the time, people who are not in full-time care are somewhere along the spectrum of the second stage.

The last stage includes severe impairment, even sometimes the loss of the ability to speak, walk, and eat, though that is not common. Incontinence is possible. Possibly few, if any, people will be recognized. Again, although this is the official line, few people actually fulfill all those predictions. Only about one person in 40 people becomes helpless, lying fetal in bed. That is not the fate of many.

The Alzheimer's Association says that over 5 million Americans currently have Alzheimer's disease and some 36 million people worldwide. The course of the disease runs anywhere from three to 26 years. Nine years is the median length of time. These figures, however, come from the date of diagnosis, which may or may not bear any relationship to the emergence of the first stage of the illness. Although the disease is not actually considered to be one of old age—the youngest person ever diagnosed with Alzheimer's disease was only 27-years-old—most people who have Alzheimer's are over 65. Ten percent of people aged sixty-five may have Alzheimer's disease, the number rising with age. One study claims that up to 47 percent of persons aged eighty-five and over will have Alzheimer's disease, but that seems a very questionable conclusion. If almost half the aged population has a disease, then Alzheimer's is not a disease but a normal condition of old age.

So, perhaps we should wait for more and possibly better studies to confirm or deny this conclusion. Who gets Alzheimer's disease? Just about anyone. It is found in all societies and in all classes and types of people all across the world, from the Western world to the South Sea Islands, to China, India, and Japan. There are some variations in its groupings – a lower incidence in Japan and a very high incidence in the Marshall Islands. Worldwide, more women than men have Alzheimer's, but this may only be a reflection of the fact that women live to a greater age than men. The younger a person is at diagnosis, the greater the tendency is for the disease to run shorter and harder.

Alzheimer's disease is named after the German doctor Alois Alzheimer, who made a study of early-onset dementia after starting out as a clinician interested in nervous and mental diseases. He worked in an asylum which housed the insane from high society families. He wanted to find the physical origins of dementia. As both a practicing physician and a researcher, Dr. Alzheimer became known for his expertise in bringing together what information he had from his patients' lives and the results of brain autopsy to make important new discoveries in the study of dementia.

Many of Dr Alzheimer's notes and interviews with patients have now been released onto the internet, together with his professional letters. All this material was uncovered recently in Germany, after being lost for many years, and can now be read in translation.

Using a newly developed, high-resolution microscope, Dr. Alzheimer found brain deterioration in those patients

43

diagnosed with dementia. He found a pattern of damage which is still considered to be the marker for the presence of Alzheimer's disease during autopsy: large numbers of senile plaques and nerve tangles in the brain cells.

These were the visible signs of degeneration in the nerve endings and the reason why the person became so impaired in functioning. Alzheimer thought that this microscopic evidence proved the presence of disease, but it was his superior and sponsor Dr. Emil Kraepelin who named this Alzheimer's disease in his own clinical textbook published in 1910. Dr. Alzheimer's own conclusions about his discovery are not shared by doctors today.

He thought he had found the cause of pre-senile dementia, a dementia which appeared before the age of sixty-five. He considered that dementias which appeared after age sixty-five were due to vascular factors and should be called "senile dementia."

Today, doctors do not make those particular divisions. They consider both early onset dementias and dementias developing after age sixty-five to be Alzheimer's disease, although this may be a decision more based on medical and drug politics, rather than on actual research. In fact, when the work of Dr Alzheimer was re-explored from 1969 onwards, it was at first the only name used to describe the dementia now called Alzheimer's disease. In the 1990s onwards, a great deal more research was done which has enabled many more findable causes of dementia to be detailed. Many of these dementias have their own name and many others are linked to specific other diseases factors, such as vascular issues, alcoholism, head trauma, Lewy Body dementia.

The term senile dementia merely means "old-age dementia," and it can include dementias with a variety of causes, some temporary and curable, others irreversible. It is a term used loosely by doctors. Dr. Alzheimer made his discovery in the late 1890s and, in 1907, wrote up his keynote case of a fifty-one-year-old woman brought to see him by her husband. She suffered various impairments and died within the year. Dr. Alzheimer conducted an autopsy of her brain and discovered the benchmark plaques and tangles. However, it was only from 1969 that the term Alzheimer's disease has been widely used.

About 50 percent of cases of late-life dementia are considered to be due to Alzheimer's disease, although current forensic autopsy studies are showing that as many as 50 percent of those diagnosed with Alzheimer's disease in life lack the plaques and tangles considered to be the benchmark sign of Alzheimer's. So, you may assume that the use of the word Alzheimer's may reduce, but that the findings of dementia will not. For caregivers, it's only a name, after all.

The different forms of dementia commonly diagnosed in the USA can be broken down as follows:

** Alzheimer's disease about 62 percent, but keep in mind that the term Alzheimer's may well be being incorrectly assigned;

** Vascular dementia about 17 percent and this includes people with Multi-Infarct Dementia, meaning they are having many small strokes, and people with too little oxygen to the brain due to blocked arteries;

** Mixed dementia, Alzheimer's Disease plus vascular issues, about 10 percent;

** Dementia with Lewy bodies, about 4 percent;

** Fronto -temporal lobe dementia, about 2 percent;

** Parkinson's dementia, about 2 percent

** All other dementias, about 3 percent.

Bear in mind, ongoing research may change a great deal of our present view of who has what dementia. A new awareness of the role of head injuries in the development of dementia, such as in sports, car crashes and wartime situations, will change what we think we know. The common ignoring of Normal Pressure Hydrocephalus

(NPH) as causing the appearance of dementia, in someone who actually has pressure on the brain from accumulated fluids, is a serious lack in present day research and medical testing. So, always read, notice and inquire further about your observations on what you're seeing in someone.

Remember too that there are also dementias considered to be of entirely unknown origin. The term "organic brain syndrome", which was formerly sometimes used by doctors as a diagnosis, is just a general term which comes from the D.S.M. IV, the bible of definitions issued by the American Psychiatric Association. The term "organic brain syndrome" has little specific meaning, other than to say that dementia is present due to causes unspecified by this extremely generalized and, therefore not very useful, term. If you come upon a doctor still using that term, better get a different doctor with more up-to-date medical knowledge about brain matters.

If your parent has been diagnosed as having Alzheimer's disease, you probably have two great wishes. One, for the cure, and two, to know the cause. There is currently no cure, although a great deal of research is being done, which is detailed later. The news is not much better when it comes to considering the cause or causes.

Right now, we have no idea what causes most cases of Alzheimer's disease. Researchers are exploring varied avenues of inquiry and, you must remember, this is probably THE most researched disease on the planet right now, so take heart. The cure could be literally just around around the next corner – this month, this year.

ALZHEIMER'S DISEASE RESEARCH
BRAIN RESEARCH:
1.Neurotransmitters:
These are the complex chemical messengers of the brain, some of which fail their duties in Alzheimer's disease. The particular failures found so far are deficiencies

in acetylcholine, with additional problems identified in somatostatin, norepinephrine, serotonin, and corticotrophin-releasing factors.

Researchers are experimenting with supplying the missing chemical to see if function can be restored and, if so, how permanently. Studies are promising. For example, lack of serotonin is connected with sleeplessness. Therefore, giving serotonin to people with Alzheimer's may be the answer to nighttime restlessness.

2. **Abnormal proteins**:

Amyloid proteins are found in abnormal quantities in the brains of people with Alzheimer's, and the production of this protein is associated with chromosome 21. Researchers are trying to discover why amyloid is produced in these greater quantities and whether the process can be reduced.

3. **Aluminum**:

The original excitement around the theory that deposits of aluminum in the brain were causing people's dementia seems to have faded, as later research seemed to indicate that there were a number of heavy metal deposits in the brains of people with dementia. It has not been established whether this is a symptom, or the cause , of dementia.

Newer research also shows larger-than-normal deposits of iron in the brains of people with Alzheimer's, which indicates a connection between the quantity of zinc in the brain and Alzheimer's. Again, no-one knows whether these are causes or side effects of dementia. Many people ask if they should stop using aluminum products. No one knows the answer, so it may not hurt. However, you are exposed to aluminum more than you might think—in antiperspirants, drinking water, antacids, soft-drink packaging. You might also reduce your intake of iron supplements and replace them with foods that are iron-rich instead.

4. **Genetics**:

There are two aspects to this question, heredity and genetics. A disorder can be hereditary, which means it runs in the family, but not necessarily genetic, which is due to prenatal factors. Both aspects are being explored in Alzheimer's research. If your parent has Alzheimer's disease, you will of course worry whether you will develop it.

However, there is very little evidence to suggest that the disease is hereditary. Only in very rare instances is there a definite genetic link, and that applies to only a handful of families. There are commonly found genetic links to dementia, involving problems on certain chromosomes, namely on 1, 14, 19, and 21. None of this makes the development of dementia a person's destiny. It takes more than a chromosome. It takes genetics, life events and other unknown factors which have not been fully established, but are still being explored.

One gene seems to play a part in the development of late-onset dementia. It is the apolipoprotein E (APOE). This gene comes in three forms: APOE2, APOE3 and APOE4. At one point, researchers were sure that the APOE4 was closely linked to late-onset dementia. However, it has since been found that even in those who do have that genetic factor, only 25 percent later exhibit dementia, meaning that 3 out of 4 do not.

As part of the research into the genetic factor, scientists have been trying to breed generations of mice that developed an Alzheimer-like disease, with some success. This is to understand the genetic component, and then concurrently, to develop drugs which will reduce or cure the disease. Even if you have a genetic factor, it only indicates an extra risk factor, not a certain destiny. Try not to worry unnecessarily.

5. **Virus**:

Some researchers are looking into the question of whether Alzheimer's has any connection to a slow virus, or to prions, which are even smaller than viruses. These studies are still inconclusive. However, there is no evidence that Alzheimer's disease is infectious or transmittable from person to person.

6. **Autoimmune Disease**:

One theory explores the mechanism of Alzheimer's disease as the breakdown of the body's natural defense system, the immune system, causing it to attack itself. Another says that the presence of toxins, genetic triggers, or trauma causes the immune system to be at war with itself. Both these theories are based on the observation that people with Alzheimer's seem to have an abnormally low level of the proteins used to fight off infections. While investigations continue, there is no absolute confirmation of these theories yet. However, anecdotally, many family members report that a parent's late-onset dementia seemed to follow trauma or loss, thus connecting it with a blow to the immune system..

7. **Dietary Factors**:

Some researchers are looking into the vitamin factor, especially the connection to B-complex deficiency, linked to Korsakoff's Syndrome, associated with alcoholism.

It is also considered that Vitamin D is a ruler of the immune system and that therefore the development of many diseases, including cancer, can be linked to low Vitamin D. Since nature and sunlight provides it best, perhaps every elder should sit in sunlight for at least two periods of fifteen minutes a day.

8. **Head Injury**:

Mayo Clinic studies have shown that one third of all people who develop what is said to be Alzheimer's Disease suffered head injuries earlier in life. At this point, many are now also looking at the number of football players, skiers and car drivers who suffered an open or closed head injury in younger years who go on to develop early-onset dementia in their fifties. At this point, too little research has been done to show what the percentage risk is in those who have had head injuries or impacts and whether in fact the damage can be prevented from causing later dementia.

9. **Life factors**:

As far as I can find, no research has been done into connections between life events and the later development of Alzheimer's. I can say, as an informal observer of life factors in those who go on to have Alzheimer's, that I could detail ten common factors. Beginning with a difficult childhood, followed by negative lifestyle issues in diet, addictions and behaviors up to old age traumas in medications, surgeries, accidents and losses. So far, dementia researchers have had little interest in these issues. As yet, all of these factors remain just questions, to which we have no definite answers.

We may find that numerous factors come together to cause the breakdown of the physical brain which we classify as Alzheimer's disease, and that we shall have to approach the question of treatments and cures on that basis, as a multifaceted campaign.

Most of the current research concentrates on interrupting the process of degeneration, since it is easier to document the actual physical degeneration than to figure out its causes. Therefore, a lot of research concentrates on developing brain chemicals to replace missing or depleted chemicals, and other drugs to promote functions which have been in decline with varying degrees of success, but no cures.

However, this is a very volatile field and has been for twenty years. Because its cause is still unknown, new theories tend to come and go and then sometimes recur with confusing rapidity. Even the very basic things we think we know about Alzheimer's are still not established beyond doubt. Here are some of the things we do not know. Despite the claims of Dr Alzheimer and the additional research since the late 1960s, there are still a number of researchers questioning whether such a disease as Alzheimer's really exists. Some of the most prominent brain cell researchers at Harvard have raised the question of whether what we call Alzheimer's disease is not, after all, merely the extreme edge of the aging arc. The problem is that we do not know enough about the aging body and the aging brain. We do know that all aging brains show signs of plaques and tangles. But, how many plaques and tangles are too many?

Where is the dividing line between normal attrition and a disease process? This is further complicated by the fact that brain degeneration and the actual dysfunction do not always correlate. People severely impaired in life have been found at autopsy to have only moderate brain degeneration, while others with severe brain degeneration were never diagnosed in life as having Alzheimer's disease. The official medical line is that Alzheimer's disease can only be truly established at autopsy, but even autopsy does not really supply that answer as clearly as we might hope.

A recent study from the VA in Honolulu showed that of 411 people diagnosed in life with Alzheimer's, about 50 percent had no signs of plaques and tangles in their brain during forensic re-autopsy and, of that 50 percent, half of them showed no signs of any kind of physical brain issues. They had perfectly healthy-looking brains. So that does raise, yet again, the question of what exactly Alzheimer's is. You may have read in various reports that there are definitive tests which can be carried out in life to establish Alzheimer's disease. The first exciting news that people with Alzheimer's have abnormally large amounts of amyloid proteins in their cells, and that this could lead to a simple skin test for Alzheimer's, has not turned out to be true. Researchers have since found that healthy people, too, have amyloid proteins in their cells.

It is very important not to let yourself be thrown into confusion by occasional sensational stories of tests, cures, and treatments. Be very cautious.

You have not yet heard the whole story. Do some of your own research into the reports and find some original scientific documentation online. Usually, such reports are culled from academic papers and then being re-storied by journalists. Those reporters may be very careless with vocabulary, often using the word Alzheimer's where the term dementia would be far more accurate. After all, all Alzheimer's is dementia but not all Dementia is Alzheimer's.

Do not go rushing all over the country, or all over the world, in pursuit of some touted cure or treatment – unless you really want to. That is a fear reaction, not a hope reaction. On the other hand, do not swallow the official line without question. The harsh fact is that the medical establishment has achieved very little in the last twenty years that has helped a single person with Alzheimer's disease or a single family. This is partly because it takes a long time to learn enough about a disease before finding treatments and cures.

However, when so little is being offered, you are entitled to do some exploring of your own. It is clear that dietary factors need further exploration. You can become a doctor in the United States without even studying nutrition for a single hour in medical school, a frightening thought considering that food is our main source of health, and sometimes a serious part of ill health. So, try healthy ideas, stay away from weird ones. If one food or drink is touted as the cure-all for everything, it probably cures nothing.

Other areas of possible exploration, available to you without harm, may include homeopathy, medicinal herbs, Chinese herbal remedies, detoxification, counseling, therapy, bodywork and exercise. These may all also supplement the life quality of a person with Alzheimer's.

Anything good for health in general will also be good to guard against dementia, but it may not provide full protection. Unfortunately, families have been discouraged from trying any experimental personal interventions while being offered little or nothing in return, except experimental drugs with high toxicity problems.

This book assumes that you are intelligent enough to make your own choices and that you want to learn about any other possible lines of inquiry, with or without anyone's approval. Just don't do any harm to yourself or your aged parent.

FUTURE TREATMENTS FOR ALZHEIMER'S DISEASE DRUGS

It is always important that you be observant of what happens when your family member starts any new drug alleged to be for Alzheimer's. Keep notes on what you see, since a variety of results are possible from any medication. Trust your own observations and always return to your doctor if negative results are observed. Since none of these drugs is a cure, but only a source of possible help, it is usually not worth going through serious side-effects in pursuit of that help. People with Alzheimer's are already compromised in health and some may be very sensitive to drugs.

Pharmacists are usually very up-front with advice because they do not prescribe the drugs and are therefore unbiased. They also have a great deal of experience of what their customers experience. They will always help with information and input. It is also very important to look up side-effects online for any drug

1. **Aricept:** (The brand name for donepezil Hcl, available since 1996)

According to manufacture, instructions, before starting on newly-available high-dose Aricept 23 mg per day, patients should be on Aricept 10 mg per day for at least 3 months. The starting dose of Aricept is 5 mg per day and can be increased to 10 mg per day after 4 to 6 weeks.

Side effects listed for Aricept are many and varied, ranging from minor to very serious. Make sure you have the list printed out by your pharmacist and pay serious attention to it. Get back advice from your doctor's office but also be prepared to make your own decision. Family experiences with Aricept vary greatly and some people really cannot tolerate the drug. Others are helped anything from a little to a lot, but most reports say that, if there are positive results, these are variable and not necessarily long term.

2. **Razadyne and Reminyl**: (The brand names for galantamine, available since 2001)

According to the manufacturers, these are for mild to moderate Alzheimer's and the range of side-effects is similar to those of Aricept.

Galantamine is an acetylcholinesterase inhibitor, which promotes higher levels of acetylcholine, which is associated with improved memory and thought. However, it does not claim to permanently improve nor does it necessarily slow down the progress of dementia. It also comes with powerful side effects such as nausea, vomiting, dizziness, headache, fatigue, weight loss and depression. Galantamine should not be taken by people with kidney or liver disease, nor those with heart disease or a history of irregular heartbeat.

3. **Namenda**: (The brand name for memantine , available since 2003)

This is for moderate to severe Alzheimer's and the maker claims that it has a low incidence of side-effects. These are listed by the manufacturer as possibly including dizziness, confusion, headache and constipation. You must inform your physician if you are suffering from cataracts, seizure disorder, kidney or liver disease, or a kidney or bladder infection, since, you might require some special tests or dosage adjustment to take Namenda safely. Namenda is intended to slow down the progress of dementia in brain processes and to help people maintain their daily capacity to carry out the normal routines of daily life.

4. **Exelon**: (The brand name for rivastigmine, available since 2000)

This is intended to help early to moderate Alzheimer's disease and it works by preventing the breakdown of acetylcholine and butyrylcholine in the brain.

Its most-common side effects include nausea, diarrhea, increased frequency of bowel movements, vomiting, muscle weakness, loss of appetite, weight loss, dizziness, drowsiness, and upset stomach. In 2007, the FDA approved the Exelon Patch to deliver this medication through a skin patch, as an option to the oral capsule.

Patients are warned never to double up the patches, as this can cause serious side effects. Family reports on the Exelon Patch cover the gamut from finding it very helpful to their family member, to the experiencing of serious side effects. As with most dementia drugs, people should proceed with caution and pay attention to the degree of discomfort being experienced.

5. **Cognex**: (also marketed as tacrine)

The Harvard Medical Newsletter says that Cognex has been associated with severe liver problems and may not be worth the risk. Especially if other drugs can do as well, with fewer side effects. Talk to your pharmacist.

All of the above medications work by affecting particular chemical messengers in the brain. They usually offer only modest improvements in memory and cognitive function in some patients. Therefore, any family would be wise to balance discomfort and bad side effects against the modest improvement likely to be seen, if at all. These are all significantly heavy medications so always consider the personal comfort level of your family member over and above the theoretical help potential.

It is not clear to me how much drug salesman are still attending Alzheimer's conferences, but clearly you should avoid sales tactics of any kind. Get your drugs prescribed by your own Alzheimer's-aware doctor, not being hyped by a salesman.

If you and your family member become involved in a drug research program, be sure to always put the personal comfort and well-being of your family member above everything else. Never be pressured by personnel involved in the research to continue when side effects and discomfort, or even just plain inconvenience, weigh down on your family.

Know that, should an effective treatment become available for dementia, it will be on the front page of every newspaper and on every television new program. You will not miss any chance to benefit.

BRAIN CHEMICALS

Since a number of imbalances in brain chemicals have been noted, some researchers have been concentrating on synthesizing the missing chemicals and supplying them. These include the following:

1. **Acetyicholine**: low levels of acetyicholine acetyltransferase (CAT) mean that the chemical messenger system of the brain is affected. Therefore, the target of many laboratory researchers is to find the replacement for the missing chemical messengers.

2. **Lecithin**: this is needed by the brain for the production of acetylcholine.

It is found in many foods, and some researchers have been giving it to Alzheimer's patients. Results are on the whole disappointing so far, but some families report success with it.

In the future, we shall undoubtedly see further development in efforts to re-balance the chemical messengers in the brain.

GENETIC RESEARCH

So much false excitement is generated around genetic research, mainly because people greatly misunderstand its real potential. Also, we may yet find that all disease is associated with genetic factors. However, since at least two types of early onset Alzheimer's are associated with gene defects, researchers are currently exploring this area.

VITAMINS, HERBS, AND DIETARY INTERVENTIONS

The last few years have seen some disappointments and even scandals around the research issues of Alzheimer's. These results simply emphasize that our present approaches to understanding this disease may be too limited and too particular—too limited in the sense that we already know but often ignore the simple ways any family member can try to help the person with Alzheimer's with the use of vitamins, herbs, and dietary interventions. Families cannot hope that drug companies are ever going to underwrite such research, since there is nothing in it for them.

Since virtually all research into Alzheimer's is being funded one way or another by drug companies, this tends to skew the research. This is why it is important to read and note all the latest discoveries on any aspect of Alzheimer's, and it is even more important to question those alleged discoveries.

Remember, the greatest amount of regular research in Alzheimer's is at present being carried out on mice. The scientific theory of this is that the brain and bodies of mice have important similarities to those of people. Undoubtedly you have observed this in your own life. No?

Ah, well, frankly that should tell you how much to rely upon that branch of Alzheimer's research. My suggestion is that you follow updates on dementia and Alzheimer's research on the internet, by regularly checking in on the Mayo Clinic at www.mayoclinic.com/health/alzheimers.

Few doctors recommend the immediate use of herbal and vitamin helpers for people with Alzheimer's, and yet it has been pretty well established over and over again—remember the wheel is always reinvented in the undisciplined world of academic research—vitamin therapy can be very useful in the treatment of dementia. This has been confirmed yet again in recent research over the last two years. The American Psychiatric Association currently recommends 1,000 IU of vitamin E twice a day for people with dementia because vitamin E leads to better oxygenation of the brain. This dosage was demonstrated to help people stay out of long-term care for an additional eight months.

Why would this work? Because stress is one of the major underlying issues—if not the major issue—in the cascade of failure which typifies Alzheimer's disease. Vitamin E, however, is not the only vitamin that seems to be of help in Alzheimer's. The B vitamins are most associated with dealing successfully with stress, but they can also be a key component in treating Alzheimer's. This was confirmed in a December 1998 article in the Journal of the American Geriatric Society that recognized that low levels of vitamin B12 are linked to the risk of cognitive impairment. This ties in with many previous studies suggesting that B complex is an essential addition to the diet of anyone at risk for Alzheimer's and possibly any elder regardless of health status.

Research surfaced in 1998 confirming the usefulness of ginkgo biloba as an aid to people with dementia. The Department of Neurology at the Oregon Sciences University in Portland, Oregon, carried out an overview study of more than two hundred studies in academic and medical publications which examined the role of ginkgo in relation to cognitive and memory impairment. They found a small but significant indication that the use of ginkgo improved impairment, which is another benefit this research has produced during the past two decades.

A further look at medicinal plants and Alzheimer's, issued by the Medical Research Council of Newcastle General Hospital in England, suggests that it is time to reexamine all the traditional herbal pharmacopeia of Western medicine.

Both Chinese and Ayurvedic medicine explore the use of traditional herbs, but Western medicine has tended to ignore this route. The Medicine Research Council suggests that in view of the few positive discoveries in the drug treatment of Alzheimer's it may be time to look further into the field of natural herbs. Both sage (Salvia officinalis) lemon balm (Melissa officinalis) have been traditionally associated with helping memory problems and may prove to be worth investigating in a more mainstream scientific protocol.

The Medical Research Council emphasizes that it is time for such research to take place, given the difficulty so far of coming up with an approved drug approach to Alzheimer's which is clearly of major importance. For the average family member, it may well be time to undertake such exploration on a personal level, consulting with your local herb store, health food store, or naturopathic healer. If you are unable to find these herbs locally, go online to find and buy them.

The most hopeful areas of drug research still continue to be those that pursue replacing or supplementing the missing brain chemical messengers that interrupt the normal functioning of the brain, both in memory and cognitive areas. This especially involves the cholinesterase inhibitors such as Namenda, Exelon and so on.

Most professionals who work with those who have Alzheimer's have often commented on the surprisingly good physical health found among the demented.

As a professional in my 24th year of caregiving people in the dementia population, I have noted this curious occurrence. I have also noticed that in general, elders tend to have only one major ailment that we might consider to be related to stress patterns in their lives—heart problems, liver disease, arthritis, cancer, and so on. If this is a valid observation, it would be logical to assume that those who have arthritis as their stress ailment do not, or rarely, have dementia and vice versa. These are both anecdotal observations. Until lifestyle itself becomes the target for researchers. However, while drug companies fund most research, we are unlikely to uncover significant life patterns that may be associated with Alzheimer's. However, this also means we should be cautious of leaping to other conclusions that are often based on isolated studies with inadequate breadth of inquiry.

Another promising development in the treatment of Alzheimer's comes from finding ways to intervene in the process of brain degeneration. A study from the Nagoya University School of Medicine, in Japan, published in January 1999, demonstrates that it may be possible in the future to block the development of Alzheimer's. Researchers concentrated on the problem of the overproduction of amyloid beta proteins found in the brains of people with Alzheimer's. These proteins are cytotoxic to neurons and are considered to play a major part in the degeneration of the brain. They are the major constituents of the senile plaques found in great number in the Alzheimer's brains.

The researchers in Japan concentrated upon using the major antioxidants idebenone and alphatocopherol to intervene in the process of degeneration by carrying out experiments on rats. They found that using these powerful antioxidants helped to prevent learning and memory deficits, which suggests that the progress of Alzheimer's could indeed be slowed or even prevented when such treatment can be developed for human beings. If we look at the latest research and writings on Alzheimer's from the medical and academic world, we can see that most exploration has moved from investigating the causes of Alzheimer's to trying to intervene in the process of the rapid development of loss, and brain degeneration.

We can also see the emergence of an interest in antioxidants and even herbal medicines as approaches to dealing with this illness. From this, it does not seem rash to conclude that there may well be natural interventions, at least at various stages of the disease. It also may be time to look at lifestyle and life habits, just as we have in other diseases, especially the diseases that impact old age. Since there is, as yet—after forty years of research—little discernible help available from medicine, it must be emphasized that everyone who hopes to avoid developing this illness should undertake certain habits that might help support the good working order of the human system.

As a decade-long observer of the lives and habits of those with Alzheimer's, I would identify' stress as the major factor.

This is even underlined in the damage found in the brains of those with Alzheimer's. Choline—the missing chemical messenger—is destroyed by cortisol, the hormone of adrenaline stress. The biggest thing most people can do to help themselves is to develop the habit of controlling and moderating their stress levels.

What causes stress?
1. **Environment** in its levels of toxicity;
2. **Diet** in the levels of stressful and unhealthy foods which cause free radicals to wreak havoc in the human organism;

3. **Emotions**, in that stress addiction is the most common addiction in the United States;

4. **Lack of exercise**, which blocks access to natural calm, emotional well-being, and spiritual nourishment;

5. **Drug Toxicity,** an inevitable side effect of the drugs most often used to treat the common conditions of old age.

Perhaps research will start moving toward a certain dim recognition that these indeed are the real issues behind the epidemic of Alzheimer's we see in the world today.

Every line of inquiry may well produce a treatment or even a cure. There is varied research being conducted, and families often find this very frustrating. Their natural desire is for a simple cause, followed by a simple treatment or cure. However, uncovering the mysteries of Alzheimer's is a very complex matter.

It involves the most complicated organ in the body, the brain, an area which medical science still knows relatively little about. It also involves examining the lives of long-lived people, which could include literally thousands of factors. Alzheimer's disease itself varies immensely from person to person, plus it is still often mis-diagnosed when either a different dementia or indeed a non-dementia health condition is involved. The research is vast, but, one day soon, we may very well read about that breakthrough from the huge amount of exploration, so never lose hope.

What's important is not waiting for medical science to stop or cure Alzheimer's. Instead, all readers should, themselves, cultivate a healthy lifestyle and bring those lessons into the lives of elders in their care.

CHAPTER FOUR

THE ALZHEIMER'S FAMILY CRISIS

"Until my mother got Alzheimer's disease, I had five brothers and sisters. Now I might as well be an only child. I've been the one to look after her. I've been the one to make decisions about her. I'm the one who never gets a holiday. They're the ones with all the opinions—and they certainly had plenty of them when it came to selling her house so she could go into care. I can hardly bring myself to speak to them now and our mother's been dead for three years." Pauline, aged forty-seven.

Unfortunately, Pauline's story is not unusual. Alzheimer's disease, because it can go on for so long and because dealing with it is endlessly arguable, can pull families apart. It is a disease of function rather than of physical body and therefore, it can cause endless dysfunction in the family itself. This is why it is very important for all family members to tackle the Alzheimer's problem together from the outset, if they can. As families deal with life, so do they deal with disease.

Given that Alzheimer's is a disruptive yet often subtle disease, infinitely variable, it tends to bring about family crisis, even in the best organized and healthiest of families. The beginnings of the disease involve gradual loss of ability to function well in life.

It tends not so much to have specific symptoms needing specific treatment. It is a disease of behaviors, and families have to make decisions about their own behaviors in response to the illness. In families with unhealthy interaction patterns, Alzheimer's disease becomes a new battleground. Even for healthy families, Alzheimer's brings many moments of crisis.

There are a whole series of difficult decisions to be made, even though the family may lack sufficient information to make them. Often, they are working without support, without help, and without any education in Alzheimer's disease and its ramifications.

The major crisis throughout is that family members are forced to revise their relationships with the person who is ill. A spouse has to adjust to loss of partnership while at the same time gradually taking on total care of someone who is beginning to function at primal levels, like a child, yet not a child.

A son or daughter must face the gradual loss of the parent as known before . It is hard for any child to take on a parental role toward a parent. To do so goes against family history with all the complications of parent-child relationships. Moreover, Alzheimer's brings additional fears to the children of its victims, as they wonder if this is a picture of their own future. It is a meeting place of loss, fear, and yearning. Many families are tied to unhealthy patterns of relating. Therefore, we can expect to find these patterns entangled in the Alzheimer world too.

Then, the care of the sick person may become a desperately embattled business. Siblings may find all their old issues revive, with unanswered needs and suppressed angers coming to the surface. A child who has seldom received nurturing care from a parent may well find it harder than most people to become that parent's caregiver. Family members who have not learned to respect and cherish each other are not likely to treat the sick person with respect, appropriate attention, and acceptance. The unhealthy rivalries and wars arise again, all fought out in the shadow of one of the most demanding of illnesses.

These battles can be subtle. Merely because your family is not actually fighting does not mean you have escaped dysfunctional patterns. The following are among the signposts of unhealthy family attitudes surrounding Alzheimer's:

DENIAL

Family members deny to each other that the situation is as serious as it really is, often treating the afflicted person as if he or she could choose to manage better. The sick family member is blamed for not trying hard enough, being too needy, or deliberately behaving badly when showing symptoms of the disease. Family members may come up with a list of elaborate explanations that deny the existence of the illness. One family, for example, talked about "Mother's nerves," not her Alzheimer's disease.

The family may deride or castigate the sick family member for exhibiting the symptoms of illness – "Ma, I told you that already "– as if the person did not have memory problems. "She doesn't even wash properly any more—it's disgusting!"—as if the sick person is being deliberately offensive.

ANGER

Family members become enraged with each other over differing opinions on
    treatment, plans for the sick person, or each other's behavior. They are unable to let go of their demands on each other or forgive each other's shortcomings in coping with the illness. Sometimes this rage is directed at the person who is sick, either as obvious abuse or more subtly as constant criticism, irritation, and demeaning treatment.

"Look, Mom, you've got to stop phoning me any time you want some little thing done. You've got to be more independent," says a son to his mother who is being overwhelmed by her illness and finding it impossible to function in daily life without help.

DESPAIR

65

A constant mood of depression and frustration may combine with grief to the point of feeling completely hopeless. Says one spouse, "Every morning when I wake up, I remember Hal's sick and then I just think, oh, let me lie here, don't let the day even start."

While it is natural for anyone to have a grief reaction to learning that a family member has Alzheimer's disease, if the feeling deepens into lingering despair, this is an unhealthy response. It is true that there is no effective treatment for Alzheimer's right now and neither is there a cure. However, there are still ways to make life feel worthwhile and emotionally valuable, even in the midst of the crisis of living with an incurable illness.

We have seen many people begin to deal with this kind of situation— people with cancer, people with AIDS—and it is time for people with Alzheimer's, and their caregivers, to begin to find better ways of dealing with this disease. Alzheimer's is a disease lived both by the person who has it and by the caregiver. When the caregiver sinks into despair, as much as we may sympathize, the situation is not being dealt with.

Caregivers must be encouraged to seek healthy coping patterns, not sanctioned to give way to unhealthy patterns. Despair is an unhealthy pattern.

BLAME

The blaming family is often found in the Alzheimer world. Instead of uniting to deal with the disease, working out family approaches and coming to a consensus, the family breaks apart. This division tends to continue for years after the crisis, separating siblings and other relatives. It happens both because there has previously been a pattern of divisiveness, but also because of the family's inability to face loss and fear.

Under the pressures of role change. Family members blame each other instead of confronting their own feelings about the disease.

AVOIDANCE

We see this in family members refusing to talk about the disease with the person who has it. A wife might say, "I couldn't possibly tell my husband he has Alzheimer's. It would really upset him and I don't want to hurt him."

This may sound considerate but it is actually the speaker's inability to reach out to the other in a painful situation. It echoes the old habit of secrecy around cancer and it condemns the real victim—the person with Alzheimer's—to loneliness and fear. The person who has the disease has invariably known for years something awful was wrong. Others do that person no favor when they deny the opportunity to speak about what is happening. Often, bizarre behaviors are triggered by family refusal to break the silence around Alzheimer's.

One man asked his support group just when they thought he should tell his wife she had Alzheimer's. "She begs me to tell her what's wrong with her and why she keeps forgetting everything," he explained, "but I don't want to upset her."

The support group facilitator explained gently that by her question his wife was giving him permission to tell her. When a person with the illness comments on being stupid, worthless, crazy, mentions that something is wrong, talks about memory loss problems, all these are clues that suggest it is time to talk about Alzheimer's. When someone says, "I forget so much," it is not a kindness to gloss it over by saying, "Oh well, we all forget things. I'm always forgetting things myself."

It is better to show understanding and empathy by saying something like, "It must be hard to forget such a lot, but it's not your fault, you know. You have an illness that causes you to forget things." Usually, people are surprisingly accepting of such news, even relieved by it.

For those who are strongly attached to the need for denial, there will still be denial, "What? Are you crazy or something?" one man retorted when his wife tried to tell him he was ill. On that and many other occasions, he accused her of being the crazy one. This was a clear message from him that he was not ready to admit the truth. Since he had always been a dominating and selfish man, this simply meant he was not about to give up control to anyone else at that point, illness or no illness.

Nothing will shake a denier, so family members need not worry that the truth will hurt them. They will brush it off. Another often hurtful example of avoidance is when family members do not come to visit the person who has Alzheimer's. Either they reduce all contacts to occasional short drop-ins, or they call from time to time on the telephone. If the person is moved into a full-time care facility, they seldom visit. When they do visit, they are reluctant to sit down and take time to listen to or be with the person.

Often, it is only certain family members who exhibit such avoidance while others carry all the caregiving burden. Such behavior may designate selfishness or emotional immaturity in being unwilling to deal with the reality of the issue, or it may indicate serious emotional maladjustment to all the issues of old age, disease, death, and loss.

"My sister never comes to see Mother. She says it's too painful. Well, I say too bad for her. Who's supposed to do the coping—nobody? Doesn't she think it's painful for me? But I'm here doing it," says one embittered caregiver, who says she will not forgive her sister.

"We're five brothers and sisters, and four of us are closely involved with looking after our dad. Our oldest brother keeps away, but he sends money when we need it.

Well, we figure that's just his way. We know he can't manage to be here. I don't know how it'll be for him later—knowing he wasn't here when we needed him—but at least we all feel we're doing everything we can," says a caregiver from a different family.

These differences in commitment certainly divide families, but the caregivers who do the best in their resolution of the Alzheimer's journey are often those who forgive the failings of others. They are the people wise enough to know that they will lose something valuable from their own lives by holding onto grudges and resentments and angers.

A common form of avoidance occurs once the person becomes more deeply impaired and is not able to initiate communication or be cognitively accurate.

Family members may say, "I won't go and see Grandma any more. There's no point. She doesn't know me."

This, of course, raises the question of whether seeing Grandma is for the family member's benefit or Grandma's. It does not answer the other question of who will love Grandma if the family doesn't. We all need love and caring and we all feel better when we get it. People who work in care homes report commonly that someone who gets good family attention shows the emotional difference. It is hard to say cognitively what the difference is, but the person is fuller, enriched, less anxious, and has less yearning when a loving family visit has occurred.

There is never a time when love is irrelevant. Grandma always needs love. Love does not mean an exchange of historically accurate data with names, faces, and times that are correct. Love means being patient, being attentive holding Grandma's hand, and maybe doing nothing but being loving. It is a pity that families so often withdraw their attention when Grandma can no longer pass the bio-data test. Even people in coma are now known to be responsive to stimulus, conversation, and people holding their hands.

People with Alzheimer's are far more conscious than people in comas. They are present. They need present love. The family that avoids visits is avoiding in the short term its feelings of pain, loss, and helplessness, but all of these feelings tend to catch up in the long run. Guilt over unfulfilled duties and omissions of love lasts a lifetime.

Not surprisingly, it often creates the dread of being similarly abandoned in need or old age. If we demonstrate that our elderly are not valued, we set ourselves up in time to also be valueless to our family members. If we show that love and caring are always valuable, we teach our children something worthwhile about loving.

THE DESIGNATED CAREGIVER SYNDROME

Sometimes there may be only one family member to care for the sick person, but more often the family somehow silently designates one member to do the caregiving, without the matter ever being discussed among them. There is no pattern to this designation. Sometimes it will be an unmarried daughter, more rarely an unmarried son, but it may also be one particular family member whether married or not, with children or not. This obviously connects with previously assumed family roles. Perhaps that person volunteered in the past to carry out caregiver roles. Perhaps that person has merely not resisted being put into the role.

However the selection takes place, the designated caregiver often is left to do all the caregiving without any practical family help other than long-distance telephone calls offering opinions, advice, and criticism. The caregiver becomes virtually deserted by the rest of the family except when major decisions are involved. Even then, he or she may not get support from the family but only input. It is not only siblings who elect a designated caregiver. Children do it to parents too.

"I look after my wife all the time and I love her very much. I'd never put her away anywhere," relates one caregiver. "But I hardly ever get to sleep through the night any more and it's very hard to take care of the house. I've got two daughters but they're pretty busy so I thought maybe I should get a woman in to help so I could get a little break. My daughters say, 'Oh Daddy, don't bring another woman into Mom's house,' so I didn't."

His daughters, however, didn't help any more than before, so the father was left alone to cope with his increasingly impaired wife. He felt that he could not risk losing the emotional approval of his daughters and therefore he was trapped as the designated caregiver. Another way designated caregivers become trapped is when geographically- distant family members deny the extent of the illness. This often happens because of the sick person's ability to cover up and put on a good social front in a telephone conversation. If those family members never come to visit, they have no means of checking out their perception of the situation. It is not uncommon for them to suggest that the caregiver is exaggerating the problems.

There are a number of ways in which the designated caregivers can prevent themselves being caught in this way, although it may be emotionally hard for them to do so. For distant relatives who do not understand the situation, there is an easy solution. Insist that they come to relieve you of duty for a weekend or a week. If proving a point is your aim, a weekend will usually do it.

One weekend spent with a person who has Alzheimer's disease is like boot camp, a thorough basic training in what the caregiver's life is really like. This has set many a family straight and ensured that at least they do not emotionally sabotage the work being done by denying the seriousness of the situation. The designated caregiver must set limits, as hard as this can be. Family members must be asked for definite times and commitments to allow the caregiver time off.

The designated caregiver must not give way on this, but should tough it out. If family members are geographically close, ask them for a weekly break, at least. If they are far away, then yearly or twice-yearly relief is not unreasonable. If children resist helping, then hire the help you need. If your money is short, ask the children to help pay for hired help.

The designated caregiver must also do as much outreach as possible into the community for additional help. All possible day-respite programs should be used. Friends should be asked for occasional help. Hiring a few hours of help a week should definitely be considered. You will find a wider range of suggestions throughout this book. Use them all.

FAMILY COUNCIL SESSIONS

Unless your family is dysfunctional in a major way, it may be hard to recognize that you are actually dealing with dysfunction.

If, however, you find that a number of the patterns outlined here are present in your family, take steps to deal with the problem. If the family is not suffering from major permanent patterns of dysfunction, you will be able to bring positive approaches to the situation. Try the family council as a way of coping, perhaps with the help of an Alzheimer's care professional. It is often easier for outsiders to bring up subjects that family members may tacitly help each other avoid.

When families resolve to deal with the situation together rather than struggling in self-destructive warfare, they can effectively meet the crisis of Alzheimer's. The following suggestions outline a way for the family to begin a campaign of coping with this crisis. This can then become a process of developing and maintaining a family plan to meet the needs of the person with Alzheimer's. There are many ways to do this, and the suggested method is merely one that you and your family could use. It has a number of components that take your family through the planning process. This plan allows family members freedom to be honest, limits tendencies to criticize or interfere with each other, and follows practical lines along which you can all plan your Alzheimer campaign.

It is necessary for family members to agree to abide by the rules outlined here. If you anticipate severe problems with compliance, you might find it useful to call in an outsider who will act as the mediator for your meeting. You may also pick one family member to play this role or simply use the outline in this book as your facilitator.

The biggest problem will be time limitations. This plan suggests very short time limits. Some families may insist on longer ones. In fact, you can take as long as your family wishes, provided everyone agrees. You can increase the times suggested here by any ratio your family needs. However, experience shows that strict time limits bring about clear planning. Adapt these guidelines to your needs. If you want to take an entire weekend for this council session, it will not be time wasted.

THE FAMILY COUNCIL PROCEDURE

The first requirement for the family council is that everyone agrees to be bound by rules and decisions. The rules include time limits for each person to speak. Each member agrees to allow the others to say their piece without interruption, correction, argument, or reproach. This allows each person to speak freely but within the agreed time. You must all agree to the following limits:

• Do not attack each other;
• Do not bring up the past;

• Do not speculate about each others future behavior;

• Respect each others differences;

Agree to abide by planning decisions on a consensus basis, which might mean that not everyone agrees in detail with everything. You all must become open to compromise in order to implement an effective plan.

FIRST STEP:

PERSONAL ALZHEIMER'S STATEMENTS

Each person has five minutes (or some other time limit) to speak without interruption and answer the following question: **What is your hope and what is your personal need in this situation?**

Some people might prefer to think it over and make notes for their answer. Here is an example of how a family answered this question. They were four children who had gotten together to discuss how to deal with the fact that their widowed mother had been diagnosed with Alzheimer's disease and was not doing well living at home alone. She had been a difficult mother for all of them, angry and often critical.

TED: I really hope that Mother can stay in her own home as long as possible. I don't want her to go into some nursing home and be unhappy there or get treated badly. On the other hand, I know I don't want to look after her. She's never shown any respect for who I am or what I want, and I can't deal with that. I guess I kind of love her deep down, but frankly most of the time I'm with her, I just feel really mad at her. I know I'd be bad at looking after her.

SUE: I want Mom to be well looked after. I don't think she's doing well at home and I'm certainly not moving back in with her. I couldn't wait to leave home and I'm not about to let go of my own life at this point. I need my space. I won't give it up for her. I still find her really hard to deal with, and she gets worse the sicker she gets.

74

BILL: I'd like Mother to stay in her own home. I know she wants that. I'll bet we can get someone good to stay with her. I don't mind coming over sometimes and staying. I don't pay any attention to her being critical. It's just her way. It doesn't mean anything. I need to know I did my best for her, and I don't mind putting some of my own life aside to help her now. That's okay with me.

ANN : I don't honestly know what I feel about our mother. I wish it was her who'd died and our father who was still alive. I'd have been prepared to have him live with us in our home but not her. She'd break up my marriage if I let her over the threshold and I want this marriage to work. I don't even know if I could help look after her at all. Since Fred and I are pretty well off, we could help financially with whatever we decide to do, but I want to physically keep out of this as much as I can.

Plainly, these family members want very different things, have very different relationships with their mother, and would probably each come to a different conclusion about what to do. However, it is still possible for them to reach a consensus that may not be anyone's best individual plan. The most important thing about the hope-and-need statement is that it really is honest and that family members do not reproach each other or try to persuade each other to feel differently.

It may seem hard to accept that some children do not love or even necessarily like their parent, but that is the reality. It is necessary to recognize this without criticism. The abuse, mistreatment, and abandonment of aged parents comes when feelings are not being dealt with honestly.

SECOND STEP:
WHAT IS YOUR GREATEST DIFFICULTY?
Each family member should take no more than three minutes to outline his or her greatest difficulty in dealing

75

with the situation. Typically the greatest difficulties involve unresolved feelings about the person—"I always hated him"—or feelings about the Alzheimer's itself.

"I'm scared I'm going to get this disease too," says Ted. "I look at Mom and I wonder if that's going to be me in thirty years. I'm kind of disgusted when I see what's happening. You know, she doesn't dress nicely any more. The house is dirty. At least I always used to respect her, even if I didn't always like her. It's hard to admit I'm judging her for being ill, but I guess I am."

THIRD STEP:
WHAT ARE THE GREATEST NEEDS HERE?
Family members should make a list of what they see as the most important
problems to be dealt with. This could be done in five minutes or less.

Conversation about the list should be kept to the minimum. A needs list might include the following:
1. help in the house;
2. daily visits from family members;
3. financial supervision;
4. shopping, laundry, and cooking;
5. coping with loneliness and social isolation;
6. coping with fear, suspicion, and anxiety
7. health and medication issues.

The lists will vary greatly. The person may need total help or occasional input. Each family member will have noticed different things that require attention, and comparing lists will help everyone develop a total picture of what is going on. The discussion will also include decisions about what are immediate needs and what can be reviewed again in the near future.

FOURTH STEP: MAKING THE FAMILY PLAN

This section is one that requires deep discussion, perhaps a lot of it. Family members should keep in mind that they need to reach a consensus, for which compromise is necessary.

Divide the plan into immediate action and future action. Under immediate action, you might suggest all the things that could be done to enable the person to stay at home, if family members agree to this. It is typical for the ultimate plan to change according to the development of the illness. It may be possible to keep the person at home with various kinds of support and intervention, then later perhaps to bring someone into the home, then to consider a small home residence placement, and ultimately perhaps to consider a dementia care or Memory Care home.

FIFTH STEP: MAKING COMMITMENTS

This is very important because differing personal commitments cause problems. The purpose of this step is to decide how to act on the needs list, either to make sure each identified need is taken care of or, in some cases, to agree to put off certain decisions until a later date.

The checklist of needs is your focus for individual commitment, but family members may also commit to other actions that are not on the list, such as agreeing to make social visits three times a week.

Each individual must state honestly the personal commitment is in time, money and actions. This will touch on all the inequalities of the family situation. One sister lives far away so she cannot give daily, weekly, or even monthly time. Neither does she have much money, so she cannot help financially.

However, there may be other ways she can contribute. Perhaps a richer sibling can pay her way to take care of Mother for two weeks a year while someone else gets time off from caregiving. Perhaps she could telephone Mother every evening for a short conversation and another sibling could pick up the bill. Together, the family can think of a number of ways of helping each other to contribute. All such offers must be based on each member's expressed wish to do something, not on pressure family members place on each other.

This is not the place to say, "Oh, yeah, Ted, you always say you'll do stuff and then you never follow through." If Ted makes a commitment and later does not stand by it, that is material for the next family council. Ted's possible future behavior is not up for discussion in this meeting. Family members have to accept each others commitment. They must not expect one member to do more work than the others merely because that person lives closest to Mother.

The family needs to work out some kind of equity based on voluntary commitment. It will not work for three members to say, "Well, Ted, we're all doing so much. How come you're not?" Each person has to commit himself, not try to railroad someone else into an equal workload. It is hard for family members to sit by while one of them simply does not make as big a donation of time, money, or effort. However this family council is to ensure that the needs of the person with Alzheimer's are met.

It is not the purpose of this meeting to make sure everyone is contributing equally. That may be the hope of the meeting, but it is not its focus. It is hard for family members to let go of their expectations of each other. It does indeed violate basic feelings about fairness when one person does a lot more than another. For that matter, it is unfair. However, being fair is not the purpose of this meeting. Carrying out an effective care plan is the purpose.

Neither is this meeting for replaying old family resentments, disappointments and feuds. This is why the guidelines suggest so many limits on time and allowing each person uninterrupted speech without comment. As hard as that may be, it is a healthy way to work through a crisis. Perhaps it will introduce some helpful new patterns of relating within the family.

A good positive way to close this meeting is for each member to write down one or more ways in which he or she will support the others in carrying out the care plan for the person with Alzheimer's. Family members might agree to make regular telephone calls to each other or have a conference call on a regular basis. S sister Sue might offer to take Ann's children to school the morning after Ann has done her regular overnight sleepover at Mother's. Ted might offer to foot the bill for certain items, and so on.

It is also an extra gift for each family member to write one positive thing they appreciate about each person present and then to read it out loud.

Although this may sound too touchy-feely for some people, the sad fact is that family members hardly ever tell each other what they appreciate, admire, or enjoy about each other. They assume others know they love them when this is often far from the truth. It never ever hurts to tell what you appreciate about an individual.

At the end of the first family meeting, a date and time should be set for the next meeting. In the meantime all family members should agree to educate themselves as much as possible about the Alzheimer journey and their own pathways as Alzheimer companions.

Some families feel the council plan would not work for them. One man said, "I know my family and they don't like the idea of being restricted in their time requirements. Does this really work?"

The answer is: It works as well as any council meetings. That means there is a basic formula for conducting the meeting from which people will constantly divert. Like your own local city or town council, as long as the actual business of the meeting is fulfilled, the time and the individual discussions can vary widely.

The real answer is that, yes, family councils work, if family members make them work. One family of four adult children made such a plan for the care of their mother. They came to her home for their discussion. It took a weekend. They often diverted from the plan but they achieved consensus. They designated an on-the-spot daughter as official caregiver, and all agreed to abide by her decisions. Two others gave monetary support and general encouragement. The other daughter, about to embark on a sailing trip around the world, telephoned in from every port of call.

In their plan they also agreed to use their mother's income and savings to pay for whatever extra caregivers were needed in order to keep their mother at home until she died. In fact, she did die peacefully at home. In another family, two sisters and a niece flew from the East Coast to meet in California with a brother and an uncle to have a family council on their mother's fate. This family also used the family council guidelines, and the majority of the members were able to come to agreement, although the brother could not accept his mother's Alzheimer's and therefore remained peripheral in her care. This continued an emotional division that had previously existed in the family. Like any plan, the family council works if people agree to make it work.

CHAPTER FIVE

ACCEPTANCE AND CAREGIVING

"No one tells you what to do for the best. Doctors don't seem to know. Leastways, ours sure didn't. People like us don't know about this thing and it's real hard to find out. I was lucky, I guess. My neighbor went through all this with his wife. When I moved in with my mother, he was real helpful to me. I sort of followed along in his footsteps. But I never felt real sure of doing right by her." Paul, 45, whose mother had Alzheimer's disease but died of a stroke.

Many people start out like Paul, not knowing what to do. Too many people end up the same way. It can be hard to find the right information about Alzheimer's disease. The biggest problem is that the help most people need is not available from medical sources, on the whole. What most people need to know is how to live with Alzheimer's, what to expect, and how to deal with the problems peculiar to this illness. Most of these problems are not really medical. Many of them are behavioral. Many of the solutions are also behavioral in that they ask changes of the family of the person with Alzheimer's.

Until people understand two things, they are in constant trouble. One is that Alzheimer's demands behavior changes of everyone living with the disease— everyone, that is, except the person who has it. Two, Alzheimer's disease varies with the person.

The biggest single problem families have is that they do not accept these two truths. They fight, deny, or ignore the changes that they must undergo, and they lock themselves into an unwinnable battle by demanding that the person with Alzheimer's change, adapt, or somehow get retrained. So the greatest part of the family's education must begin with education about the person who has the disease.

If you are a family caregiver, you are already an expert in this area. You know the person you are dealing with. You know what upsets that person, what pleases and what enrages. You know what that person can do. You know that sometimes, even though you do not understand why, that person's capacity to manage is greatly reduced. You probably know how to bribe, persuade, and cajole successfully to get your way most of the time.

So you are already an expert in one area of Alzheimer's. Your first piece of education is to acknowledge that you are an expert. No doctor, nurse, or social worker knows your person like you do. You might try noting down the things that you know about dealing with Alzheimer's. In fact, it would be educational for you to keep a daily journal. It will help you to get a grip on things and it will be a valuable record. If other people become involved in caring for the person with Alzheimer's, your journal will help them to know what works, what usually happens in certain situations, and how to deal with events.

Such a journal need not be elaborate. You do not have to be a writer. Just jot things down. You will probably become aware of many more things as you do this.

It is also useful to learn as much as you can about the disease itself. In one way, this will not be easy since you probably already know more than most people. It is also true that we have very little real incontrovertible information available on this disease. You can learn about its typical behaviors, however, and this knowledge will help you and your family avoid battles you cannot win.

Although each person with Alzheimer's exhibits the illness in a very individual way, there are some general guidelines you can learn. One is that the symptoms of Alzheimer's can vary literally from day to day, usually according to the general condition of the person. They do not, however, vary hugely. A really big drop in functioning in any way points to a medical emergency of some kind.

You do not have to know the kind to take action. Get your person to the doctor as soon as possible. If necessary, take them to the emergency room, if their doctor is not available.

"I don't understand my mother," says Tom in despair. "One day she's fine. She can dress herself and put all her clothes on properly. That's normal for her, right? Then suddenly another day she can't do any of those things. I tell her to put her trousers on and she lays them on top of her thighs. She sticks her blouse on upside-down. I mean, what's going on?"

Probably what is going on is that Tom's mother is less well on her days of coping badly. This doesn't mean less well with Alzheimer's disease. She may have a cold or a touch of flu, a gastrointestinal problem, pain somewhere in the body, or maybe some emotional upset has happened. Any disturbance of health or emotional well-being can disrupt the Alzheimer patient's ability to function. In fact, ill health may show up only in increased malfunction.

In order to really learn from the person you are looking after, you need to be able to step back sometimes and be an impartial observer. That is not always easy, especially if you are angry or overtired. However, you will be better able to deal with the problems of caregiving if you can keep your role as observer. The biggest source of aggravation for a caregiver is the feeling that the person with Alzheimer's is deliberately doing things, or not doing them, to annoy, manipulate, or punish. Actually, each of these intentions would require the kind of rational ability to think things through that people with Alzheimer's specifically do not have.

To be the impartial observer, you need to be educated about who you are as a caregiver—especially about your emotional vulnerabilities and your personal stress reactions. Again, a journal will help you to learn about yourself as a caregiver and enable you to watch out for the ways in that you can be caught up in the stress of the situation. There is no need to blame yourself.

We are all human and as caregivers we all have our shortcomings, especially when we are tired or upset. But just to know yourself will help you make the appropriate allowances, for yourself and for the person you look after. As part of your education about this disease, read the problem-solving section of chapter 7, which will cover many of the intricacies of dealing with Alzheimer's that often only caregivers know about. Another way to learn more is to attend as many workshops, training classes, and seminars as you can find.

There is, unfortunately, a dearth of practical knowledge being given out in workshops, unless a caregiver is presenting the workshop. Too many deal with new medical research and the latest drug-testing experiments, subjects that do not relieve families where they most need relief. But go anyway and be prepared to ask questions. If you have particular requests, make a note of them before the workshop or seminar so that you will not forget them or be too intimidated to ask.

Contact your local branch of the Alzheimer's Association, or go on line, to find out where support groups meet. Support groups are an important source of information for you. Caregivers know who the good doctors are, ways of dealing with problems, and the area's resources. They also know all the daily grind and its hardships, in a way that only caregivers can. It can bring you relief and a sense of peace just to be with people who know this situation.

Other parts of your education will include research into financial and legal issues. A husband and wife with shared resources need to look into safeguarding their assets, ensuring that power of attorney is taken care of, and doing their estate planning for the future. Unfortunately, until the health care system in this country is revised considerably,

Alzheimer's disease can bankrupt a family. Forward-looking planning of the right kind can help to alleviate some of the financial burden. In the past, some couples have divorced simply so that they could protect their assets when one of them needed full-time placement in a care facility.

Therefore, it is very important that you see an expert in this field. Usually that will be a lawyer with expertise and experience in elder law and elder estate planning, with special reference to issues of providing for long-term health care. Be sure the person you see really is an expert in these issues. Check out references and recommendations from local organizations—for example, the American Association of Retired Persons (AARP), your local Area Agency on Aging, elder services agencies, and senior centers.

When you do find someone who is recommended, do not be shy about asking what experience that person has had in such estate planning. You want someone who has dealt with hundreds of clients needing such a service, not a handful. Be ruthless about your questions, because this professional can make or mar your own future financial well-being.

Many experts suggest that you do not allow this person to also handle investing your finances.

If your family member has not yet had a diagnosis of Alzheimer's, that person might still be eligible for long-term care insurance. You obviously cannot get such insurance after the diagnosis, but you might get it before any suspicions you have about your family member are actually confirmed.

Be extremely careful about any such insurance and seek guidance from an independent adviser. Do not take out policies on the advice of your insurance agent alone. Take time to think things over and have the policy looked at by an independent expert. Ordinary health insurance will cover normal hospitalization even if Medicare does not, and few other policies cover long-term care which includes Alzheimer's disease although many claim to do so. The national headquarters of AARP reports that there are many spurious long-term care insurance policies around. When the crunch comes, they avoid paying out just when you need them to do so. Alzheimer's disease is covered by very few policies, so be suspicious and do not let yourself be talked into anything. Your local senior centers, senior services agencies, and AARP branches can often help you with this matter.

If you are facing possible future placement of a family member, do not assume that you need either to have long-term care insurance or to pay down to ruin.

It is not true that you cannot keep your family member on in an assisted living in which he or she is already comfortable after resources have been spent to the level at which time Medicaid takes over. Many reputable care places are part of a federal aid program that allows them to keep a resident on after the patient no longer has full financial resources. Such facilities get federal grants in return for being part of the program. You can get this information in advance and choose your facility accordingly; picking one that guarantees keeping your relative on once Medicaid kicks in.

Do not imagine that residents on Medicaid are treated any differently from those who are still paying full rates. They are not. State regulations these days ensure that every resident is treated with the same respect and gets the same care and attention. If this were not so, the institution could lose its license. Remember, however, that money does not buy certainty when it comes to good care, so do not be too attached to having to pay for everything yourself. As part of your education for the future, learn about the range of care in your part of the world. Read Chapter Eleven on placing someone in care so that you know well ahead of time what your alternatives are. Not everyone with advanced Alzheimer's disease has to be placed in a skilled nursing facility. Look around at small home care residences so that you have a good idea of other choices well ahead of making any. That way, you will not be caught by surprise or rushed into a decision you may regret.

Learn about the possible course of this disease, while also acknowledging that it can vary greatly. That way, you will recognize certain changes as they happen. For example, you will notice when vision changes cause a person to be unable to center on a chair or toilet seat and be ready to help act as a guide. You will be alerted then that you should probably be around your relative when he or she goes up and down stairs, just to keep an eye on safety hazards.

Knowing what is happening in the disease course will help you be much more accepting. For example, when you begin to realize that your relative is no longer connecting words with their meaning, you will not get angry when your questions or commands are not carried through.

"I told Miriam to switch off the light before she left the room. She nodded but she didn't do it. I told her six more times before I got mad at her and just went in and did it myself," says Paul, still angry as he tells the story.

He will not win such battles because he is fighting the disease. Miriam no longer knows what Paul is saying when he uses nouns whose meanings are lost to her. If he pointed to the objects represented by the nouns he uses, she might get the meaning. Such education keeps you sane. Another good way to keep sane is by educating yourself about good caregiving and about caring for yourself as a caregiver. This is very important. The biggest problem for caregivers is the drop in their own health due to stress. This is often the most- neglected aspect of caregiving. Caregivers put themselves last, but unfortunately that only guarantees that they will not be effective in their task. Make sure you go to any stress management classes you can find. Often, such classes are offered at senior centers, in recognition of the fact that life in old age can have many stresses. Do not dismiss these classes as if you could not learn anything useful. Take exercise classes, especially gentle exercises like yoga and Tai chi. Learn about your diet and what it should consist of as you age. All of these things will be part of your education for survival.

Other ways of educating yourself could include learning how to communicate better, especially if your relationships with your family members are not going well. If you are an elder yourself, you might have learned ways of communicating (or not communicating) that do not serve you well any more. Relearning such habits and finding better ways to do things and talk about things will form part of your network of help. Basically, people only know what you tell them, and sometimes you have to learn how to be specific. You may need to brush up your habits of communication.

If you are caring for a member of your family, it is likely that you will be involved in that person's death process. If you know nothing about the process of death and dying, consider attending workshops or training courses on the subject. If there are no such workshops near you, there are very helpful books available.

They are listed in the Bibliography at the back of this book. Read ahead of time so that you can become aware of how you feel about death and dying.

Be open to learning from experts how to cope better with life. Life with Alzheimer's has many burdens, so do not scorn getting help, guidance, or a chance to talk things over with a counselor, therapist, or psychologist. Do not think that only people who are crazy would seek such help.

It is common now for people to seek counseling when they are dealing with difficult situations. Talking things over with a professional can help you to see a situation more clearly. In the old days, family members were around more and could talk things over. Now many people do not even have a minister, priest, or rabbi to discuss life difficulties with, yet life has become incredibly complex. So allow yourself to get that extra help and input where it can do most good.

How can you determine whether a counselor could help? Take a look at this list:

1. I feel trapped and helpless.
2. I am tense and unhappy every day.
3. I can't face the day when I wake up.
4. I can't sleep.
5. I feel so guilty every time I get angry.
6. I don't know who to turn to.
7. I don't think I can go on much longer.

If any of these statements describe how you feel, you could undoubtedly get help from counseling. To find a good counselor, ask your local senior services agency. Ask your doctor for references. Check out any local counseling offices or services. They are usually listed in the Yellow Pages under Counseling or Therapy. It may take one or two attempts to find the person you feel most comfortable with, but you will benefit from counseling. How many times you go is up to you. You will work it out with your therapist. Counseling does not have to be long term or even very expensive. You will probably find that your health insurance covers at least part of the payment.

You must also educate yourself about the effect of medications on your relative. Once a person is manifesting Alzheimer's disease, the norms for body response change, becoming highly variable and individual. Drugs are never tested on people with dementias, except in the case of specific drugs for Alzheimer's. This means that no one can say how a particular drug will affect a person who has Alzheimer's disease. The side effects that might be minor in reasonably healthy people can be devastating in Alzheimer's patients.

You must do two things to safeguard your relative. First, ask your doctor what the side effects of any new medication are, according to the manufacturer. If your doctor does not know, ask the pharmacist to give you printed information on side effects.

These are usually provided by the manufacturer. This way, you know what to look out for. This is very important since your relative probably will not be able to tell you, "Oh I feel sick," or "My vision has gone blurry" You will have to watch for unusual behavior from your relative. Keep daily notes after any change of medication so that you have a documentation of new behaviors or troubling developments. Do not accept the doctor's assurances that they are not due to the medication. Ask your doctor to test by withdrawing the medication to see whether behavior becomes normal again.

The second thing to do to safeguard your relative is to demand a change, reduction, or cessation of medication if drastic changes occur. Here is a family anecdote with a message. Albert had severe Alzheimer's disease and was regularly becoming very agitated at night. His wife, Sybil, mentioned this to his neurologist who then prescribed Haldol, a frequently prescribed medication in cases of Alzheimer's agitation. If Sybil had asked the neurologist what the side effects of Haldol are, she would have learned that among them are confusion, memory loss, and tendency to falling.

(You might think therefore that Haldol would not necessarily be the best choice for an Alzheimer patient, but that is another story.)

Albert became even more agitated, and the neurologist doubled the dose. He became more agitated again, and the neurologist increased the dose once more. Albert became violent and unmanageable, and his wife committed him to an Alzheimer unit. There, Albert's medication was immediately reduced and gradually tapered off altogether within the next three weeks. Albert never at any time became violent or even agitated. From this, his new doctor at the nursing home concluded that Albert was actually allergic to Haldol, as are most elders with dementia. If Sybil had been better informed and aggressive in determining what was going on, possibly she need never have put Albert into care.

The lesson here is to be demanding and to insist upon the validity of what you observe. You are not, unless you are a doctor, an expert on medications, but you are an expert on what is the usual behavior of your relative. You do not have to accept disadvantageous conditions that come about through medications. Since extremely little is known about the effects of medication on people with Alzheimer's, you are the resident expert on its effects upon your relative. Keep notes and be firm.

This brings us to the conclusion of this education campaign, which is intended merely to reinforce something that you may not have realized: you are the expert. You are the one who really knows the person with Alzheimer's. Even if you do not always know the best solutions for ALL your problems, you are still the resident expert. Dealing with Alzheimer's disease is such a divisive process that it seems appropriate to look at ways in which we can bring everything back together.

Families can become wretchedly fragmented over dealing with Alzheimer's, because of the difficulty of caring for the person who has the disease and because of family members' individual ways of interacting. Perhaps the most important fact for families to accept is that there is no perfect, no absolutely right, no unarguable way to deal with this disease. Every family's passage is inevitably going to be marked by disagreement and uncertainty.

Family members can often become very attached to their individual points of view. That is understandable, but underlying this attachment is often the secret conviction that doing things the "right" way will somehow change the course of Alzheimer's disease. This is what underlies so much of the anxiety and guilt among families affected by the disease.

"I just wish I knew the right thing to do," says Mitch of his father. "You know, if I could just make the right decisions then perhaps it'll stop what's happening."

Alzheimer's disease is an internal process. There is a level at which outer conditions affect it, but its main course is something within the victim. No one else can take it away, stop it, or even slow it down. Within each person, it has its own path and its own paces responding to some internal timetable. Of course we should make life as easy and as comfortable as possible for the person who has this illness, but we need to accept that it is the other person's illness. We need to accept the present.

"I want my mother back," says Manny. "I don't want her to be this helpless little woman. My mother was strong and she looked after me and I want her back."

Manny's sense of loss and pain is understandable, but he cannot ever have that mother back. Either he accepts taking on the role of becoming father to his mother, or he continues to rage and sorrow about his loss. Because he does not cope, he fails to keep his appointments with social workers and others who could help him and enable his mother to have better care.

Many people with Alzheimer's consistently fail to get their needs met because their families are locked into trying to maintain who they used to be. One man tests his wife's memory every day to see if she can recall the names, addresses, and telephone numbers of their children. He is

92

thrilled when she can but devastated when she fails. Actually, it is irrelevant whether she has a good memory on Tuesday—she definitely has Alzheimer's every day.

The person with Alzheimer's can have a great deal of happiness in the average day—but experiencing that happiness depends a great deal on the family. A lot can be done to make the present enjoyable for all concerned. Family members are often much sadder than the person who has the illness. The one good thing about Alzheimer's is that you can rely upon the here and now, although it can seem bizarre, especially if someone is under the impression that he is living in a time forty years ago.

But bizarre need not be a problem. Happiness and sadness are the problems. Anxiety and grief are the problems. If we love only the person who used to be, the person here and now gets no love from us. This is a very common situation in Alzheimer families.

No one loves the person who is here now. That may seem a harsh way to describe the family's sadness and sense of loss, but it is nevertheless true.

When we say, "How can we help?" we have entered present time. We have stopped being trapped in the past. We have stopped fighting the disease and the person in the disease. We are ready and able to help. That is the start of reconciliation. We continue it by staying aware every day of what we are learning and how we are growing.

This enables us to avoid being caught up in recrimination and struggle. We can learn to appreciate our own abilities and forgive our shortcomings. We are reconciled with who we are. Many people tormented by the Alzheimer situation are really being tormented by their own inner feelings of rage and guilt.

If we cannot accept our anger—the natural feelings that sometimes say, "I wish he were dead," or "How much longer is she going to live?"—then we become obsessed by guilt. Accepting our inner feelings allows us to come to oneness inside, instead of being torn apart by all kinds of opposing emotions. This is the powerful spiritual journey of caregiving. It forces us to be honest and it asks of us to accept and forgive ourselves and others. Acceptance and forgiveness are very important for the future of the family. Make no mistake—this is a disease that divides families forever, not a passing crisis soon over.

A quick crisis can bring everyone close, but a long-term struggle allows each person to behave according to personal patterns of behavior. One will be a caregiver, someone else will be the organizer, someone else again will be the one who disappears whenever needed. If family members cannot learn to accept each others levels of functioning, they may never speak to each other again. It is hard for the one who does the caring to forgive those who do not, but it is less work in the long run. Holding grudges uses up valuable energy and some people manage to make the decision not to use their energies in that way.

Those who hold their anger close will be constantly torn up within; many stay permanently angry with Alzheimer's itself. Again, while understandable, this anger is a waste of time and energy. Alzheimer's is just a disease. It happens. Unfair things happen and we learn to cope or we don't. We can choose to do either. The person interested in reconciliation will choose to cope, finding a way of making sense of the ordeal of Alzheimer's. We tend to be reluctant to accept another person's ordeal and in Alzheimer's, family members often project a sense of suffering that is not really there for the person who is ill. People suffer from imagined suffering much more than from suffering itself.

Following are some of the ways in which family caregivers have expressed their different views on making sense of the Alzheimer's disease.

"In the end, my mother was just like a child. That was hard for us. She'd always been so competent and able to

94

cope. Then there was this childlike clinging little girl. But, you know, she told me things then I never knew before. I learned that she had been frightened badly by her father. She used to come up to me and say, 'Don't let my daddy hurt me.'

"And I used to hold her and assure her she was safe. And sometimes I used to think maybe this is what had to happen for her to finally find safety and love."

Marguerite, aged forty-nine.

"One thing that happened when we looked after our granddad was that my high school friends just loved him. He'd come out with some really weird, garbled ways of saying things and they loved that—they said he was like a mad poet. I thought that was kind of neat." ADAM, aged nineteen.

"My mother was always a real nag. She worried about everything. In the early stages of her illness, she was just awful, so anxious all the time. Later she was so relaxed and happy. She'd sit out in the sunshine smiling in this blissful way. I could see she'd come to some place where she was more peaceful. Of course, she'd forgotten all the things she used to worry about. Even her hypertension got better." Dick, aged forty-two.

The issue of reconciliation becomes much more complicated when the initial relationship, prior to the illness, was a troubled one—when children, for example, are dealing with a sick parent who had many shortcomings as a parent. For some people, this is simply not an issue they can deal with.

"I can't look after my mother. I wouldn't put her into a home, but I'd never look after her myself. I just can't. She was never there for me as a child. She never behaved like my mother. She was always out working. She was a social worker and she spent all her time at work. I was looked after by hired girls. I can't get over that. ' Maureen, 62.

Maureen, fortunately, is wealthy. She pays an extraordinarily high wage to a caregiver who looks after her mother. She is doing the best she can and certainly she is obtaining the care her mother needs. Whether holding on to her anger and resentment will ultimately serve her is an issue she may come to deal with later.

Rosie took a different path, although some of her story is the same.

"I could never stand my mother. She was always an angry, resentful woman who obviously didn't want to be a mother," she recalls. "I left home as soon as I could. I never went back until she was sick. Actually, I didn't know she was sick. I went to visit her for the first time in four or five years and I found her whole house in a squalid mess. It was really clear she couldn't manage."

Rosie got her mother to a doctor. After a long series of medical investigations, her mother was diagnosed with Alzheimer's disease.

"So then I had to think about what to do. It just seemed that there wasn't much choice at that moment. So I moved back in and started looking after her. Well, it was horrible. I still couldn't stand all the ways she was just like she used to be—and then there were a whole lot of new ways I couldn't stand either. She really drove me crazy. Well, it's kind of hard to explain but it just took up so much of my energy that I knew I had to let go of my anger, and somehow change. And I did. I changed. I just kind of let go of all those feelings I had about her. I hadn't got the strength to hold on any more to all that stuff."

From that time on, Rosie and her mother developed an entirely new kind of relationship. "We became kind of like bad girls together. We'd go to the zoo sometimes or we'd sleep in late and not do our washing up till next day. The more I kind of relaxed, the more she changed. She even got quite a sense of humor. It was like she forgot what was bugging her all those years. And she forgot me. She could never get my name right. Once she said to me right out of the blue, 'Oh you should meet my daughter—she's a lovely girl,' and that was just great. I can only say I'm really glad I tried and it was really okay. My mother's dead now but I really feel good about what I did and how our life was in those last couple of years."

Rosie finally had to put her mother into care, and that was also a difficult choice.

"We were traveling at the time and she woke up one morning and there was nothing she could do. She couldn't dress, couldn't go to the bathroom, and couldn't eat even. I felt real scared then. I knew it was over for us at that point. Well, I found a home for her, a small house where five old ladies lived. Her Social Security covered the cost and she fit right in. It was kind of a warm, down-homey place. I knew she'd be okay. I knew we were okay."

Another aspect of reconciliation that will concern family members is to make some reconciliation with the disease itself. Otherwise they live in terror of it for the rest of their lives.

"Every time I forgot my keys, I thought, 'Oh God, that's it— it's happening to me now. I'm going to be just like my father.' I felt so scared and angry," relates one son.

These fears are extremely normal—and so too are those memory lapses. Losing keys, forgetting where you parked the car, searching for glasses—those are the usual memory lapses everyone experiences, including young people. But young people do not usually immediately think of Alzheimer's. Older people do.

A person could spend twenty years worrying about Alzheimer's and get run over by a truck at age fifty-five before the disease manifests. The most valuable thing each person can do is to fully develop his or her potential to live the fullest possible life and to work to overcome personal problems and issues. There is nothing else that we can really aim for that makes sense. As it happens, working on ourselves in this way, at emotional, spiritual, and intellectual levels, also makes us into more lovable people, and lovable people, if they need it, attract good caregivers.

This is not entirely a frivolous suggestion. In a fifty-four-bed Alzheimer care unit in the San Francisco Bay area, the residents who got the most love were the ones who were most lovable. They were easygoing, had a good sense of humor, were appreciative of others, and responsive to other people. These are characteristics that serve anyone well, in Alzheimer's or out.

One major reconciliation that family members need to undergo is one our whole society needs—the ability to cherish other people for their capacity to love and care, not for their intellect or power. Instead of being attached to our rational ways of valuing others, we need to develop our ability to love the other exactly as he or she is. This is not easy. Partners get disgusted with spouses who are demented. Children are frightened by parents who are no longer fully rational. We value people's independence and separateness. We need to learn to value what is there—the child that emerges.

"I learned to look at my husband a whole new way," **Alice** recalls. "I had to or go crazy. He couldn't run our life any more the way he used to. I had to do it. He got to goof off and do nothing or mess about, and I hated it. I wanted him back. I wanted the old age we had promised ourselves—our golden years of travel and fun."

Alice's husband became quite childlike. He wanted toys from the toy store. When his grandsons visited, he took their toys and refused to give them back. Finally, Alice gave in and bought him some toys of his own.

"And you know, one day I was watching him and, I'm really not a Christian, not a churchgoer, but I thought about that thing about being as little children and I said to myself, that's him. That's my Bill. And the funny thing is, once I could see him as the little boy he must have been, I felt as if that's who he was—a sweet, untouched little boy. It was like that part of him wasn't sick at all. Children don't get Alzheimer's, do they? I loved him in a new kind of way after that.

"He wasn't my husband any more but it didn't hurt quite as much because, after all, I still had him—that lovely boy."

In sacred writings, this emergence would be seen as the divine child who remains untouched by darkness or sickness. For many caregivers this is one of the deep reconciliations that can come about.

"I looked after an old lady for a year," says one caregiver. "She wasn't a relative but I felt about her as if she were my grandmother. Even more, I could see the little girl in her—the way she wanted her daddy sometimes, the way she asked to go home to her daddy's house. I cherished her as if she were a little girl then and I didn't find it demeaning at all. She was a little child sometimes, just as we all are. Only it wasn't hidden away any more in her. You could see it."

Accepting the emergence of the child can be the most difficult thing for family members to do. Grown-ups are often disconcerted by childish or childlike behavior in adults. They are embarrassed at the betrayal. They want not to see it. And yet in a way it is one of the most whole parts of the person with Alzheimer's disease. With the emergence of the child can come a new sense of play, an emotional openness, a willingness to try new things and be real and authentic in all feelings, an ability to be free of judgment. It is also an area that allows great healing, even within the disease process itself. Many people have suffered somewhat or greatly as children. Most people, throughout their lives, are working and reworking their primary relationships within themselves.

This never stops until death itself. Particularly in old age comes a deep reworking of the primary issues of love, abandonment, wounding, and healing. This is why so many older people are preoccupied with their early lives. It is a normal part of maturation and reconciliation in life, of coming to peace. It is exactly the same for the person with Alzheimer's, who is also deeply involved in those primary relationships, still trying to work them through and reach peace within. The main difference is that the person with Alzheimer's has often actually forgotten that those parent figures are dead, that this is some entirely different year from the one they are thinking about. That difference is not really as great as we might think. For most of us, the parent figures remain alive within us in the ways we play out our lives and our major relationships.

When the person with Alzheimer's reveals that he actually expects his mother to come home that night, the caregiver often focuses on the time error caused by dementia.   We can help by concentrating instead on what is being said about the parent. We can focus on the feelings about the parent and the unresolved issues being talked about. We can help most of all by becoming an ideally loving parent figure so that the longing for love and safety and acceptance—common to all human beings— can actually be fulfilled in the here and now. By giving unconditional love now, we help heal the long-ago wounds of the past. By helping in that great healing, we give the same message to ourselves:. No matter what the wound, we can all be healed. We are learning about the deep nature of healing in the latter half of this century.

We have all been brutally reminded that, after all, not all disease can necessarily be conquered, not all healing means recovery or even survival. We are being forced to ask ourselves how we may be healed. We have been learning that not all healing means not dying. Sometimes it means finding peace before we die.

CHAPTER SIX

ALZHEIMER'S COMMUNICATION:
FOLLOWING CLUES

There is a science and an art in every human communication, and both are needed when dealing with people who have Alzheimer's disease. Basic communication is heavily impaired in this disease, presumably because physical damage to the brain impedes normal message-passing in the brain system. It becomes hard for people to formulate and express complex thoughts, and rational thinking is obstructed.

This shows in many ways. The person mishears or misinterprets what is said. The meaning of words may be disconnected from their sound. Even if the person hears accurately, it may be impossible for the person to construct a logical sentence for reply. Even if the capacity to think cognitively is present, the speech center of the brain may not obey the person's wishes and the wrong words may emerge, as happens to stroke victims.

We may never know which of the communication processes is actually dysfunctional, because the person may be unable to reply intelligibly or may suffer from "word salad," speaking a stream of apparent nonsense. These obstacles can lead to many roadblocks in normal communication. In fact, the person with Alzheimer's is like someone dealing with a damaged computer. Parts of the program are missing, and without the support and structure supplied by these missing bits of programming, the person is left trying to make sense of a world that seems crazy The single most important thing to remember about all this is that the person with Alzheimer's disease is not crazy.

Every communication has a purpose, and our task as caregivers is to find out what that is. Nothing is meaningless—no word, no action. Even what sounds like nonsense, even the continuous repetition of the same sentence or question, is intended to express a feeling, to show a need, to give information, or to get a response. As caregivers, we need to remind ourselves constantly that Alzheimer-afflicted people are trying to understand everyday life, just as we are.

We all want to make sense of things. That is the basis of most therapy— to make sense of our story. If strange or distressing events happen to us in daily life, we ask ourselves what is going on. If people behave in puzzling ways, we ask what they mean by them. People with Alzheimer's are doing the same thing. The difference is that an essential part of their information system has been disabled. It is like being a stranger in a strange land, not understanding the customs nor speaking the language very well. Having Alzheimer's is like becoming that stranger without having consciously or knowingly gone into unknown territory.

Instead, everything that is familiar and loved about life becomes strange, unknown, and therefore often frightening. Even people we love become strangers, since we may not be able to name them correctly or place them in context. Staying aware of this as a central issue of Alzheimer's communication helps remind us to always ask ourselves: "What is the need being expressed by this behavior?" When language and function betray the sick, leaving them without the ability to say what they mean, the only thing left is action.

Acting out becomes a symbolic portrayal of their truth. For example, people who constantly wander away from home may be acting out the fear they are trying to flee or the displacement they express by going off to find "home" again. People with this disease are constantly acting out their needs and their feelings within a fractured brain structure. This means as caregivers we often witness apparently bizarre behavior or are confronted with peculiar demands.

Stressed-out caregivers often fall into blaming the person at this point, simply because the complexities of communication are too overwhelming, added to everything else that has to be taken care of.

As one wife said, "You know, there are days when I really don't give a damn what he needs. I just think, he's okay because he's got me, but who cares about my needs?"

That caregiver's reactions are very understandable. Why indeed should we bother so much about what someone with Alzheimer's really means? The main reason is that the sick person will inevitably continue to react negatively if his or her needs are not met and thus will increase the caregiver load. This is not, by the way, deliberate on their part. It is an instinctual reaction, just like the sunflower following the sun. Therefore, our task is to decode the communication and to meet the need being expressed.

Caregivers could use this mantra: No Alzheimer communication is meaningless. This applies whether the communication takes the form of words or actions. Most caregivers report the highest amount of stress arises when the person they are looking after is behaving weirdly.

In many workshops, caregivers find resolution once they begin to comprehend what certain speech and behavior might actually signify. Even in care facilities—and sometimes especially in care facilities—the real expressed needs of the person with Alzheimer's are virtually ignored. Being unlistened to is one of the major factors in creating what are usually described as problem behaviors. It is often the main impetus in outbreaks of violence when they do occur.

In years of dealing with Alzheimer sufferers in private homes, home care residences, and skilled nursing facilities, I have never come across a problem behavior that did not arise from unmet needs or poor handling by caregivers. This aspect of Alzheimer care is neglected, undoubtedly because no one likes to criticize a caregiver who is already overburdened. However, it is time to talk about this, since ignoring this central issue actually leads to most of the major difficulties in caring for a person with Alzheimer's. The sufferer feels alone, and this result in what others define as difficult behaviors, which lead to most of the placements into full-time care.

It would probably be useful to drop the term "difficult behaviors" since that phrase makes them the fault of the person who is sick,instead of reminding us that there may be better ways for us to listen, observe and respond. Searching for the meaning of the behavior pays off, sometimes dramatically, and helps families to relate better.

One woman reports, "My mother drove me crazy by always asking where the children were. I'd tell her, and then she'd ask again. Eventually I realized this was her only way of being able to start a conversation. It really just meant she wanted to talk."

Once this woman was able to see her mother's annoyingly repeated question as a sort of verbal "ahem," it no longer bothered her. Most Alzheimer sufferers feel alone trying to communicate what they want and feel. Some family members may find it hard to give time to solving behavior problems and, in many other cases, dealing with the real issues of communication may involve more honesty and risk than family members are willing to face. This is understandable, but if they do not make the effort, they will certainly become overwhelmed by caregiving.

It is common for people with Alzheimer's to drop the use of nouns altogether, including personal names. Often a sentence comes out sounding very gnomic indeed because of the lack of nouns. For example, one woman said after a walk, "The little ones are very tired." At first, her caregiver thought she meant she was tired, but then the woman rubbed her foot painfully and repeated, "These little ones are tired now."

When the caregiver removed the woman's shoes, she found that her toes had been skinned by ill-fitting shoes. The "little ones" were her toes, which were sore.

These constant roadblocks to communication are wearisome to both parties, and it is caregiver weariness that leads to most Alzheimer placements into professional care. It is not because people need such care—in fact, skilled nursing care is often extremely inappropriate for dementia patients.

People are put into care because their caregivers are worn out. They are put into care because families cannot deal with the real issues of their illness, typically undealt-with anger, grief, secrecy about the illness, unaccepted role changes, control problems, and inability to nurture.

This chapter takes the widest possible interpretation of communication, acknowledging what linguists and social researchers tell us—that only 30 percent of human communication is verbal, and the rest is symbolically expressed through body language, actions, and behaviors. Begin your understanding by listening to what the person says and responding or interacting kindly.

When you speak with a person who is deeply impaired by Alzheimer's, speak in sentences that are clear and simple, in a voice that is soft and kind, in a manner that is unhurried and relaxed. Sharp voices agitate. Hurry causes nervousness and dysfunction. Complexity causes intellectual overload, which will bring about a distress response that could be rage, tears, anxiety, or extreme slowness and inability to do tasks.

Speak on the same level as the person, both literally so you can be face to face, and figuratively so that you express ideas in a way that can be easily absorbed.

No one likes to be patronized, and people with Alzheimer's resent it as much as anyone else. As caregivers, we always need to remind ourselves that, just because people have Alzheimer's disease it does not mean they are either insensitive or stupid. They are functionally impaired, not stupid, and they are often highly self-aware.

They may sometimes say things that we would consider inappropriate and hurtful— "Oh, you're very fat, aren't you?"—but this is due to unlearning the societal inhibitors they were taught when young.

Be sure to approach the person from the front so you can be seen. Surprises are not welcome in the world of dementia. Speak clearly, give plenty of time for the other person to respond, and avoid memory questions. To be sure you have the person's attention, gently place your hand on his or her arm, hand, or shoulder and be sure you have eye contact. Persons with Alzheimer's often spend periods of time in altered consciousness and they need to be gently brought back into the here and now.

It is astonishing how many caregivers think it**appropriate to ask a person with severe memory problems all kinds of questions involving memory. Here is, unfortunately, a typical family dialogue.

"Hi, Ma, how are you? Do you know who I am? No, not Vonnie, that was your brother. Why would you think I was your brother, Ma? Do you know the names of your other children? Huh? Well, what did you do today, Ma? What did you have for breakfast? Look, do you know who this is? Huh, Ma?"

If this man could accept his mother's Alzheimer's disease, the greeting might be much less distressing for all concerned if it went as follows: "Hi, Ma, it's me, your son Ron. Good to see you. Boy, you look pretty nice today. Let's see, it's about five now. They'll be bringing your dinner soon, so let me show you some photos we took last week."

This communication works better because it does not constantly put Ron's mother to the test. It also considerately supplies linkage and potentially missing information and it keeps emphasis on the here and now. The photographs will give Ron a chance to identify other important family members and to remind his mother that they exist and they love her. The past is a murky country for the Alzheimer's sufferer and the future has often become unimaginable, but the present is always with us.

Therefore, we can always rely on the present to be a part of our communication that can be fully shared. Just as when we meet a stranger at a social gathering, we need to introduce ourselves afresh each time we meet a person with Alzheimer's disease. Here is another common example of a distressful communication:

"You remember me, don't you? Can you tell me what my name is? Do you remember what we did last week? We really enjoyed ourselves. Don't tell me you've forgotten already."

This would be much less distressing rephrased as, "Hello, Irene, I'm Sally. I met you last week at the center and we had a lot of fun dancing together. My goodness, you're a really good dancer, aren't you?"

Relatives too should learn this social skill of introducing themselves. This will help to remove some of their distress when their husbands or fathers or mothers cannot get their names right. It is not personal, not an attack, but merely due to the disease.

Conversational chit-chat can remain as a good social skill even among the deeply afflicted. This can lead distant family members to assume that the person is in better shape than he or she really is. A typical family miscommunication along this line might be as follows:

Mary: Mom, this is April on the telephone.

Mom: April?*

Mary: Yes, your daughter April. She's my younger sister.

Mom: Well, who are you?

Mary: I'm your oldest daughter. Now, come on, April's here on the telephone.

Mom heads into the kitchen because she has no idea what the word telephone represents anymore. Mary retrieves Mom and leads her to the telephone. Mom puts the wrong end of the receiver to her ear and Mary puts it the right way up.

Mary: Say, hi April, Mom.

Mom: Hi, April.

April: Oh Mom, it's so good to hear your voice. You sound great. How are you doing?

Mom: I'm doing fine.

April: So did you go to Henry's for Thanksgiving?

Mom: Yes. [Actually she did not.]

April: That's great. Did you enjoy yourself?

Mom: Yes.

April: Well, Bill and I are fine and... [April chats on, Mom gives one word responses].

Two minutes after this conversation ends, Mom has forgotten entirely that there was a call, and April is telling Bill that Mom sounds fine and she cannot possibly be doing as badly as Mary always says she is.

Memory:

A number of other major problems in communication concern memory issues. Most of us do not really understand how deeply we are tied into our memory structure until we live with someone who is not. Then we see that the loss of reliable memory function fractures the whole of life.

Caregivers who are confronted by this often find themselves frustrated, sometimes hurt, and often caught up in uncomfortable exchanges that result in bad communication. These appear constantly in the questions raised by caregivers in Alzheimer workshops: "My dad has no idea what year this is. I think he thinks it's about 1925 and he calls me by his brother's name. What should do?"

The major loss in memory dysfunction is knowing what year this is. Memory is like a ship, anchored to the current year. When it loses that anchor entirely, due to short-term memory damage, we never know from one moment to the next what year that person's memory has drifted into. To the person with Alzheimer's, memories feel as real as experience of the here and now.

Rather than designating this as a delusion, it is more useful to consider it as a loss of reference system. When confronted by a parent whose memory ship may have floated back to age sixteen in Texas, your acceptance can be very calming.

If an adult son explains that this is 1993 and he is not his father's younger brother, this information may not be acceptable or understandable. It may seem as if a time machine has suddenly landed from the future. Experimentation is the answer. If his father can accept gentle reorienting to the here and now, that is good. If he does not accept it or seems uninterested, then the son needs to accept his father's drift of memory.

One area of communication that puzzles and often hurts family members is their misidentification. A son is thought to be a brother or father. A daughter is called sister or mother. Wives are thought to be mothers. Husbands are called Daddy. These misidentified relatives feel rejected and hurt. However, if they could put themselves into that frustrating Alzheimer brain, they might see that, first, the ability to label a person correctly has been destroyed. Second, if the memory ship has drifted to the past, to premarriage days, then it makes sense that they cannot be spouse or child in that particular memory picture.

Third, when they are named as the parent, the person is really saying, "I love you and I need your love and care and protection as a child needs his parent."

When they are named as a sibling, the person is saying, "I know you. You're family."

Confrontation as communication leads to hostility and misunderstanding and never achieves what the caregiver wants to achieve, which is usually either to stop the person from doing something, or alternatively, to make that person do some desired action. Usually when confrontation occurs, it comes out of the caregiver's anxiety, hurry, or hostility and these are probably additional reasons why it fails. Persons with Alzheimer's are very sensitive and they pick up even underlying unstated angers and fears.

Instead of confronting, think of how you would get a small child to cooperate. You would be kind, persuasive, and patient, ideally. Use these same skills and make sure you always allow enough time. Instead of saying, "No, you can't do that," use diversion, bribery, and food. Say, "I really need you to help me over here right now," and lead the person away from danger or trouble.

If you have confronted the person, with unwanted results, ask yourself if you were actually feeling hostile at the moment you did it. Maybe you were. In our hurry and need, we sometimes forget to treat people we look after with dignity and respect. We want to demand instant obedience and get the situation over and done with.

Another major communication problem in families is the big question of whether to tell The Awful Truth. This is often raised in workshops and support groups. A husband asks, "Should I tell my wife she has Alzheimer's disease?"

A wife asks, "When is the right time to say something to him about his illness? I don't want to hurt him."

Family members mean well when they say nothing. They fear that they will hurt, frighten, or depress the person concerned, and so no one ever mentions the dreaded word Alzheimer's. This kind of thinking has been pretty much exploded now in other medical fields. Numerous studies have shown that people not only want to know what is wrong with them, they are actually relieved to hear the truth even when the news is bad. This is as true in Alzheimer's as it is in cancer, Huntington's chorea, and other serious illnesses.

People are so stressed by knowing that something is wrong, even though no one talks about it, that the truth is a great relief and a great release. There is absolutely no chance that a person who has been slowly developing Alzheimer's over the years has not noticed that something is terribly wrong. Usually, in the past, before Alzheimer awareness had developed, people thought they were either going crazy or becoming unaccountably stupid.

However they described it, they knew without a doubt that something was profoundly wrong with them. If we never speak of the illness to them, we condemn them to live in a lonely place of silence. If we want to be good caregivers, we will release them from being so alone. Caregivers who refuse to tell the truth need to look deeply into their own motivation, beyond the expressed wish to spare someone else pain, into the problem of their own pain.

Nowadays, most people working in the Alzheimer's field meet people who have already accurately suspected that this is what is wrong with them. Although it is frightening, they are relieved to be able to speak about what is happening, and they can then try to develop ways of dealing with some aspects of the disease. The caregiver who tells the truth is not taking away hope. In fact, those who wish to deny their illness will manage to do so in the face of all family insistence. It is impossible to take away denial from those who really wish to hide behind it.

As people become more deeply impaired by Alzheimer's, they find it harder to complete the tasks of daily living. They often need constant verbal cueing to do things like get dressed or take a shower. The main thing to remember about any such cueing is that it must be done one step at a time. Memory failure means the person cannot keep a number of actions in mind. Give one instruction at a time and point to the objects you name: "Here, Annie, why don't you put on this sock? That's it. That's great. Now this one. Good. Now here's your sneaker. And here's the other one."

Constant conversational accompaniment can be very soothing. Never give orders, always make suggestions. Never insist. Always back off if there is a problem and return to it in a few moments. Never try to hurry anyone through step-by-step procedures. Hurry causes dysfunction. If the person resists a procedure, ask yourself if this is necessary and drop it if it is not.

If it is essential, try bribery. A dish of ice cream, a cookie, or a piece of cake can be a soothing communication device. Be specific—for example, "Here's some great strawberry ice cream," not "What kind of ice cream would you like?" Never offer more than two choices. Preferably the conversation should be referring to an actual object in the room. The danger of referring to absent objects is that you have no way of knowing for sure that the words you use are being understood by the person you are speaking to.

A sample of this confusion from my own caregiving life.

"Hannah, I've made some really nice lentil soup today. Would you like some?" I said, but without showing Hannah the soup.

"Oh yes," says Hannah enthusiastically.

Given a generous serving of soup, Hannah eats with obvious and increasing reluctance and distaste until I ask:" Is there something wrong?"

"Oh yes, it's terrible, just terrible!"

Since the soup was actually delicious, I realized that lentil soup was simply something that Hannah did not enjoy eating. Checking with a family member confirmed that Hannah had always hated lentil soup.

A more constructive exchange would have been the following.

"I made some great lentil, soup, Hannah. What do you think about having some,"

I could have asked her while showing her the pan of soup. Even then, maybe I should actually offer a taste, in case she doesn't recognize what kind of soup it is.

Most impaired people cannot choose appropriate clothing for the day, yet it is nice to involve them in the process of picking what they wear. Show, for example, two sweaters and ask, "Would you like this one or that one today?"

If you do not want to deal with choices, then offer items with a strong suggestion that manipulates toward your choice.

"This sweater always looks so pretty on you, Hannah. Would you like to wear it today?" will usually elicit the answer "yes."

In the same way, when your charge asks you difficult questions that lead to problems, you will soon learn how to evade, concur, or be conversationally noncommittal. This may cause dilemmas for you at first. Most of us want honesty in our communication with others. We do not feel good about lying, rightly so. However, in dementia, we are often presented with situations that specifically bring up issues in which blatant literal honesty causes great pain and confusion. For example, a weeping eighty-eight-year-old woman says, "Why hasn't my mother been to see me? I haven't seen her for a long time."

Even if told the truth that her mother is dead, she will usually reject the information because she is not living in the present reality, and you cannot make her do so. If you believe that reality orientation is the one honest way to go, you may tell this human being who desperately needs mothering that her mother is dead. This is neither necessary, relevant, nor kind, and it tends to bring about catastrophic reactions of grief or rage.

It is profoundly necessary for caregivers of people with dementia to understand that we must respect their reality. It is not their duty to come into our reality. It is only the inexperienced, rigid, or unkind caregiver who sticks to ramming unpleasant so-called "real" facts down the throats of lonely, frightened old people. No one can forcibly change the reality of a person with Alzheimer's. Often, the demented person knows emotionally exactly what is needed and will not be distracted from that need.

The displaced one wants to go home, even if he is sitting in his own home. The one who feels useless and unwanted wants to cook dinner or clean up the house that is no longer hers and may not even exist any more. The frightened lonely one wants Mother. Just as small children only want what they want, with a deep emotional intensity, so too do those with Alzheimer's. Reality orientation is meaningless because they are expressing their feelings, not concerns about facts.

A perceptive and kindly caregiver soon begins to learn that dealing with the emotional needs presented by the person is a much more useful way to go. To the woman who wants to know where her mother is, the caregiver might say, "I'm not sure right now [this will almost certainly be true], but maybe you'd like to have some coffee with me and we can sit and read together., or even

"I guess you're really missing your Mom right now, huh?" and then being like a mother to this person.

To the woman who says she is expected at home, the caregiver might say sympathetically, "Are you feeling lonely right now?" or "I guess you're really missing your family right now. I'm sorry" then offer some attractive distraction.

The basic rule in communicating with people presenting their own demented reality is, first, acknowledge their feelings and, second, do something about their needs, either in offering emotional support and security or by distracting them into something that helps them let go of the feeling for a while.

What about the person who is offering an entirely different reality in the form of an interesting fantasy life? This is not uncommon, though it is more usual for people to go back in time, either to traumas that tormented them or, more commonly, to happy times and pleasant events. In the case of people who basically are simply reviewing their lives and coming to resolution, n caregivers need only offer empathy and support.

One woman in a day-care program repeatedly told the story of her first day at school when she wet her pants and was humiliated by the teacher in front of everyone. Some caregivers regularly laughed at this, reinforcing her feelings of humiliation. Others belittled the story—"Oh, you worry too much, Elsie"—thus denying her feelings.

It does not take great perception to understand several things about Elsie's story The first important point, which none of the caregivers picked up, is that the day-care experience was in itself triggering the memory—new surroundings, new faces, insecurity, fear of humiliation, probably actual fear of not getting to the bathroom in time.

Second, because the caregivers were failing to respond appropriately to her need, Elsie was condemned to repetition of her story. I suggested to the care staff that a more useful response might be an acknowledgment of her feelings, followed by reassurance.

"Oh, Elsie, what a terrible thing to happen to you on your first day at school. That teacher was wrong to treat you that way. She should have helped you. It's quite different here. We're your friends here and I'll show you exactly where the bathroom is. You needn't worry about that."

Caregivers need to be ready to respond appropriately however often the story is told. It is not memory loss that causes Elsie to repeat her story, except in a superficial sense. It is the continuing pain and fear she still feels, even 84 years later. Take care of her needs at the feeling level and she will no longer need to repeat her story. It will be exorcised, leaving her free to return to more pleasant memories.

Many people stick with their happy memories. One old lady who lived in a nursing home gave birth to babies every night. She was overcome with joy and triumph, and her happiness was so clear to the staff that eventually everyone joined in and supported her. Staff would look in on her and say, "How's that baby coming, Grace?"

This brings us to the dilemma of re-created reality. It is one thing to agree to support people's feelings about real events in the past and even to accept that they are re-expencing those events in an emotionally real but not factual sense in the present.

However, a number of people with Alzheimer's may create an entirely new past and present. Again, we could label this with psychiatric jargon as delusion and hallucination, but that does not get us anywhere, except to give us a vocabulary A vocabulary does not, however, give us the tools to deal with the person. For that we need not words but our own feelings of empathy.

When a person who has been diagnosed with Alzheimer's seems to be experiencing actual hallucinatory incidents, it is a very good idea to get a closer diagnosis which accounts for this. Most Alzheimer's is not psychiatric, but it is not unknown for a person with dementia to also be suffering from mental illness, usually of much longer course than the Alzheimer's. More rarely, we will find that a persons aid to be suffering from dementia is actually only experiencing a mental illness and no dementia. There is far more awareness of this issue these days and it is important to get more focused help for such a person, usually described as having a dual diagnosis

People besieged by Alzheimer's go through great pain, fear, and loss at various stages. Therefore, when we see them creating brand-new interesting and rewarding fantasy lives for themselves, we should recognize this as a coping device, a way of making the unbearable bearable—even a way of telling the self an interesting story, making a new life when the old one was not fulfilling many needs. We all need to dream. Having Alzheimer's does not remove this need, although it may remove the cognitive ability to divide dream from actuality.

There are probably more people in care homes and facilities with these mixed issues than people at home. That is because emotional and spiritual life in such places is much more bleak for those forced to live in them. They are taken from a real life of their own, however impaired, and given instead a restrictive regime devised by someone else and modeled on a sterile medical mode of containment. Often people have nothing or little to do in such places, so they create their own amusement.

One 84-year-old woman I knew, Rosie, was married once, widowed and childless. In an Alzheimer's unit she developed a rich new life in which she had been married seven times and had twenty-one children and was currently pregnant.

Another woman in that same facility, Maria, was 95, a devout Roman Catholic with a large Mexican family who seldom came to see her. Soon after being moved into the facility, she began carrying around a doll that she said was the Baby Jesus. Richard, a man who had always done many home repairs, walked around the Alzheimer's unit where he lived, carrying out invisible tasks of repair. He even took an invisible dog for walks sometimes. His actions were so authentic that one nurse swore she could almost see the dog.

Some professionals feel that people with dementia should have their invented realities adjusted to factual life, forcibly if necessary However, this can never be done successfully. It seems far more humane and considerate simply to accept their reality.

Most professionals who work with people with dementia adjust to accepting their reality, if only because the residents hold on to it so fiercely that any attempt to take it away only causes tears and tantrums. In rare instances, re-created realities cause problems, as in the case of the man who felt that neighbors were about to break into his house, whereupon he became very violent. However, his fears arose out of the terror and loneliness of his disease, which his wife refused to discuss with him, and also possible wartime-caused PTSD.

Good parents do not tell young children they are liars when they come in with stories of talking dogs and friendly giants and adventures flying on butterfly backs. We understand that they have imagination and a story they want to tell. We owe at least as much understanding to those who are working through their dementia in ways that bring them pleasure or consolation.

People with dementia have two needs of us in our communication with them. They need us to respect the adult in them as well as to honor the child. Instead of feeling, as many family members do, that it is demeaning to see an adult operating in some aspects at a child level, perhaps instead we can come to understand that the child within does not get Alzheimer's. Therefore, if we can work with the child that emerges as the disease progresses, we can ease the pain and loneliness of this difficult journey. If we can acknowledge the physics professor's new ability to paint as freely and inventively as a child, instead of bemoaning the fact that his great computing mind is damaged beyond repair, we can do more for him in the average day than everyone who mourns the lost professor.

We will get the cues in the language those with Alzheimer's use to us. If the impaired adult wants mother, father, brother, we know he feels lonely and insecure. If he asks to go home or back to the Texas he left as a youth, we know he feels lost and displaced. If we can find ways to offer the accepting and unchanging love of the ideal mother, father, brother, if we can create a world that welcomes him and helps him feel at home, that person will be much happier and much more resolved.

Language may fail gradually as the disease progresses. The person uses names less often, if ever—something that may happen even in the early phases. Nouns used abstractly may not be connected to their meaning any more. The person may be unable to find the words needed.

"Could you buy me one of those—you know—small and I had two in my refrigerator but now there's only one," turns out to be a request for lamb chops—which, by the way, the caregiver understood. Language connections may be lost, either because of memory failure—the inability to hold a sentence in mind so it can be completed—or because of brain dysfunction, so that rational thoughts literally cannot go through the right neuropathways. Sentences may stay uncompleted or become very convoluted as the person follows around determinedly but cannot get quite the right words and phrases.

119

"I think that something soon will happen that is terrible if something soon is not done," was Hannah's way of saying "I urgently need to get to the bathroom."

As caregivers, therefore, we will make intuitive jumps, guesses, and mistakes as we try to understand. If someone really cannot tell us what is wanted, we can try to be empathetic. It is important to let that person know we really want to understand the frustration. If we cannot understand, finally, we can say, "I'm really sorry I don't understand what you need. I'll try harder."

Gradually, the impaired person may say less and less and seem to be further and further away. This awayness, which is certainly some kind of being in an altered state, often goes on for longer and longer, especially toward the end stages of the disease. None of us knows where people go to in these states, but we do know from brain studies that people with Alzheimer's dream much more than most people and also show a great deal of brain wave activity, especially in the right hemisphere.

The insensitive person may simply say, as one man did of his mother, "There's no one home anymore. I mean, she's just dead really. She's a living corpse."

However, most caregivers who develop a good understanding of the Alzheimer process do not agree with this estimation. Instead, they tend to say, as one nurse did, "I don't know where she goes but I know for sure she goes somewhere. I sit next to her and I can see that she's far away. Then she comes back and she's there again."

More people need to understand that right hemisphere activity is more heart and feeling centered. People operating from right hemisphere are more intuitive, more able to experience spiritual awareness and vast connection with the sense of oneness that mystics experience. They feel music and art and joyfulness from these and for many life at this later stage can indeed be very joyful. This sense of interior preoccupation is often found in those in the later stages of Alzheimer's. They give the impression, not of being the living dead, but of being the absorbed absentee away doing other things. It never seems to be a distressed state, always one of quiet absorption.

Some people in such states have even been taken to the hospital, as one Jungian therapist with severe Alzheimer's was, only to be sent home diagnosed as being in an altered state.

If someone seems to be in this state, usually shown by being very deep in thought and unaware of the here and now, it is good to sit quietly and await the person's return. It is better not to interrupt or break into this state of reverie, since that can be experienced as disruptive or frightening. Their awayness should be respected. You can even explore it by asking the person where he or she has been. The answers can be interesting, though not necessarily very comprehensible.

Use physical contact as your constant message that everything is all right and that you love the person. It is rare for people to find such touch unwelcome.

For most people, touch is a message that gets through when words do not. Lay your hand on the person's arm when you talk, gently rub her back, massage his shoulders, give a hand massage. Any such physical movement should be slow, firm, and leisurely. Quick pats and tugs are very disturbing and unpleasant. If a hug is appropriate and welcome, a side-by-side hug is less threatening than a full frontal body hug, which can be very invasive. Do not use hugging as a way of patronizing people. They will detect your insincerity.

Some of your communication may concern the setting of limits. It is important to be able to set limits, even if the person cannot remember them. It is appropriate to say to someone who is being verbally abusive, "I'm sorry you feel like that but I don't care to be spoken to this way." Such words do not necessarily stop the person with Alzheimer's, but they will make you feel less powerless.

Setting limits is not the same as trying to retrain someone. Forget about that entirely. Trying to retrain someone with Alzheimer's is one of the things that family members find hard to let go of.

A husband reports, "I tell her not to go into the kitchen, but she's always sneaking in there, and I can't trust her anymore."

The answer is not to forbid the wife the kitchen in which she has worked for thirty-five years. It is to make the kitchen Alzheimer-proof.

A wife says, "My biggest problem right now is trying to get my husband to stop answering the phone when I'm out. I keep telling him."

Yes, but having Alzheimer's means he keeps forgetting. Her solution must be not to change him but to turn off the telephone ringer and get a quiet answering machine. The basis of all our communication in Alzheimer's disease should be empathetic understanding, receptivity, intuition, and loving kindness. If we use them all constantly, we will understand much, reach out more, and become the true companions that are so needed and yearned for by those who journey through this darkness.

The key to the puzzle usually lies in listening with the heart. To think, not in terms of control and giving orders, but in changing ourselves so we understand better.

CHAPTER SEVEN

IS IT REALLY ALZHEIMER'S

Much has changed in the last ten years in both the diagnosis of dementia and the slow recognition that there are a number of other specific dementias that may well have been diagnosed as Alzheimer's in the past, but in fact are not. This exploration still continues and we will undoubtedly find that our present knowledge expands further, but meanwhile here are the dementias commonly identified and often found at this point.

It is also worth noting that Alzheimer's may well have been carelessly diagnosed in the past. Recent forensic re-examination of the brain of people diagnosed in life with Alzheimer's reveal that many of them had not had Alzheimer's disease at all, since there were no signs of plaques and tangles in the brains and these are considered to be the identifier of someone having had Alzheimer's disease.

A forensic autopsy study carried out by the VA in Honolulu and published in 2011 revealed that of 411 people diagnosed in life as having Alzheimer's disease, 50 percent did not. They had no signs at all of any plaques and tangles in the brain. Moreover, one quarter of that number had brains in which no signs at all of any disease, damage or dysfunction was physically present. In other words, they had very healthy-looking brains.

What does this mean?

It indicates that, presumably, their dementia originated from some health condition centered elsewhere in the body. Or maybe from medication interaction. So, although Alzheimer's is still the most spoken-of dementia, it may well not in reality be the most common dementia at all. Also, in the past, medical investigators were not always paying sufficient attention to whether someone alleged to have Alzheimer's might not actually be suffering from a serious mental health issue, not Alzheimer's dementia at all. It is not unusual to find an elder, said to have Alzheimer's, who is actually a life-long paranoid schizophrenic or has a bi-polar disorder, or is even suffering from a PTSD condition resulting from life events, in wartime, in childhood or resulting from other traumas.

Every family member should at least be aware of these issues since, right now there seems to be uncertainty and error in the diagnosing of Alzheimer;s disease to a significant degree. Sometimes we laypeople really do have to do something like our own research and insist on further and more accurate diagnosis. We are not the experts on disease, but sometimes the experts are not as accurate as we need them to be to really help our own family member. And sometimes accurate diagnosis is not easily made anyway. Alzheimer's is largely diagnosed from the appearance of symptoms which are behavioral and functional and which are also commonly found in a great many other conditions. Hence the confused diagnoses which can occur. Never forget that the so-called Alzheimer's work-up commonly used to make diagnosis is not really an Alzheimer's diagnosis at all, or only by default.

The work-up actually searches for other possible physical causes of the symptoms presented. It looks for heart trouble, liver problems, medication issues and so on. If none of these are found, then comes the diagnosis of Alzheimer's dementia. It is only a default diagnosis. It is not definitively a finding of actual Alzheimer's disease.

If a definitive marker is able to be found in life, then diagnosis will become more error free. Right now, the definitive marker – the plaques and tangles of Alzheimer's – can only be found at autopsy. And new research is showing that plaques and tangles are actually being discovered in autopsies of people said to have other dementias. So, just be aware that our knowledge of the dementias is increasing at such a pace that more and more information is coming through. Awareness of other dementias is increasing , as is the ability to actually find physical evidence that supports diagnosis. This picture will continue to develop and change as clinicians develop awareness and tools for diagnosis. So, we can continue to expect many more facts that will clarify the dementia situation in medicine.

We are likely to see a much more definitive diagnosis of Alzheimer's as research continues on this issue. Or we may well find that Alzheimer's becomes much less commonly spoken of, while other dementias become more accurately recognized. Be sure to keep up with these issues. They will appear in newspaper articles, on TV and undoubtedly all over the internet. There is no more-researched disease on the planet right now than Alzheimer's. The whole of medicine is with you on wanting the cure.

Meanwhile, what are those other dementias we are hearing about? The following is a section on the most commonly mentioned now, but remember that research continues and that medical research finds new information all the time.

The Other Dementias

1. Lewy Body Dementia (sometimes written as Dementia with Lewy Bodies).

It is increasingly common now to find that people with dementia are being diagnosed with having Lewy Body Dementia. Some medical resources claim that this is the second most common dementia diagnosed today, after Alzheimer's.

It is certainly true that more people are being diagnosed with Lewy Body Dementia. The Lewy bodies referred to are abnormal proteins found in regions of the brain that control thinking and movement. The development of Lewy Body dementia shows up in thinking, memory and, often, the appearance of colorful hallucinations that may often be the first sign of Lewy Body Dementia.

According to the Mayo Clinic, further signs may include:

Movement disorders, such as developing a shuffling walk and muscle rigidity, or muscle tremors, as is   found in Parkinson's disease;

Memory problems, as are found in Alzheimer's and other dementias;

Sleep problems, which might including physically acting out dreams;

Concentration problems, including having periods of confusion, staring into space and reduced ability to express thoughts in speech.

It is also being recognized that the Lewy Body type proteins are also found in Parkinson's and certain other dementias and that research on these issues is very much in its beginning stages. Expect to see more developments in the next decade. which may well change our whole view of dementia.

More information and help is available from The Lewy Body Dementia Organization at **http://www.lbda.org/** also at www.mayoclinic.org/lewy-body-dementia/

2. Frontotemporal Dementia

This is a dementia associated with change and deterioration in the health of the frontotemporal lobe of the brain. This in an area associated with personality, behavior and language. The onset of this dementia may be in the 40s, a younger age than most dementias. It may manifest with behavior changes, including loss of impulse control, personality changes and a further range of deterioration such as language loss and lack of understanding.

126

In the past, before it was being recognized as a dementia, it was often considered to be a psychiatric condition, rather than being connected with physical changes in the brain. It could also include loss of inhibition, compulsive over-eating and language losses.

Other developments may include aphasia, loss of understanding words and meaning and difficulty finding words and even complete loss of ability to speak. It can also include movement issues such as changes in gait, tremors, muscle spasms and weakness, poor co-ordination and swallowing difficulties.

Some forms of frontotemporal dementia resemble what used to be called Pick's disease, but others differ greatly from that. Its origins are largely unknown, since genetic research indicates inconsistency in producing clues and it does not seem to run in families, as Huntington's Disease does.

Research continues and more information and help is available from the The Association for Frontotemporal Degeneration online at http://www.theaftd.corg and the online Frontotemporal Dementia Caregiver Support Center at http://ftdsupport.com/

3. Vascular Dementia

Vascular dementia, as the name implies, is a dementia which comes about as the result of impaired blood blood flow to the brain. This can be due to strokes, high blood pressure, high cholesterol, damage from a long term smoking habit or other causes and also the accrued damage from many tiny strokes.

The presence of this dementia shows up in memory impairment, thinking process problems, including trouble with making decisions, loss of rational thinking and more. It can also include changes in gait and balance, agitation, urinary incontinence. It is often confused with Alzheimer's and can be determined by the full-Alzheimer's workup which will show the accrued damage from blood vessel issues through CT scans and MRI s

More help and information is available online at http://www.stroke.org and from the Mayo Clinic at www.mayoclinic.com/health/vascular-dementia/DS00934/

4. Wernicke-Korsakoff Syndrome

Wernicke-Korsakoff syndrome is a brain disorder most often associated with long-term alcoholism, in which brain dysfunctions occur because of a thiamine deficiency (Vitamin B1) over a long period of time.

This longterm deficiency results in permanent physical damage to the central nervous system (brain and spinal cord) and the peripheral nervous system (the rest of the body). It may also include symptoms caused by alcohol withdrawal. Heavy alcohol use obstructs the breakdown of thiamin in the body.

Outward signs of this can include behavioral changes, severe short-term memory issues, poor physical co-ordination, possibly unusual eye movement, difficulties in decision-making and choices, increasing signs of dementia affecting whole-brain abilities. And probably there will have been behavioral evidence of alcoholism.

5. Parkinson's Disease

The Parkinson's Disease Foundation defines Parkinson's as a movement disorder which increases as time goes by. Its origins are unknown, but it increases in severity as vital nerve endings in the brain deteriorate and die.

Typical movement issues include :

a) tremors affecting hands, arms, legs, jaw and face ;

b) bradykinesia, the slowness of movement that we see in people who have Parkinson's;

c) rigidity or stiffness of the limbs and body;

d) balance impairment and co-ordination.

Later in the course of the disease, people may develop dementia, sometimes called Alzheimer's and sometimes Parkinson's dementia.

There are many encouraging developments in the care and treatment of Parkinson's and you will find this information at the following on-line sites: The Parkinson's' Disease Foundation at www.pdf.org;; Michael Fox, famed as an actor and as a young-onset Parkinson's victim, has a lively site on all the latest research and treatment at
www.michaelfox.org..

The Mayo Clinic also offers a thorough review of disease and treatment options at mayoclinic.com/health/parkinsons-disease/DS00295 .

Other commonly discussed dementias you might want to look up include:

Huntington's Disease, Down Syndrome and Creutzfeldt-Jakob Disease which is also nicknamed Mad Cow Disease. You will also find the term Mild Cognitive Impairment being used to describe a non-progressing dementia that looks like the early stages of Alzheimer's but which may well not intensify into a more disabling form of dementia.

And it would be wise to assume that, as research intensifies more, you will be hearing about other dementias, other causes of dementia and other treatments and perhaps, as we all hope, cures for many of them.

CHAPTER EIGHT

DAILY PROBLEM-SOLVING

Sometimes caregivers feel as if the whole of caring for someone with Alzheimer's is one problem after another.

It can sometimes be true that the caregiver's main task is the constant search for solutions. This chapter will help you look for ways of coping with problems. Sometimes, solutions may be obvious or they may require some innovative thinking or adjustment on your part. Not all problems necessarily have a solution that puts a stop to them. The answer sometimes will be to try to change yourself.

There is only one major thing to remember: All Alzheimer behaviors have meaning. Your task as a caregiver is to try to find that meaning and meet the need expressed by it. This can sometimes be difficult. After all, this disease is a dementia. However, the person with the dementia is always trying to make sense of an increasingly bewildering world. The resulting behaviors are intended to communicate.

Brain function impairment gives rise to certain patterns of behavior, such as repeating questions or constantly pacing about, but the exact nature of the behavior usually represents a need the person is trying to express. Children do that too. Little children who fidget and grizzle because they cannot say, "I'm tired."

Take a typically irritating behavior. Many people with Alzheimer's ask repetitive questions. "What time is it?" or "Can I go home now?" or "Where are my mother and father?"

These questions may be repeated over and over because the person cannot remember asking the question and getting an answer. However, as you will see in the section headed

Repetitive Questions , there is often a deeper issue involved. When you uncover this deeper issue, you may find you can stop those irritating questions. The secret is that, when you meet the real needs of the person with Alzheimer's, you will find both resolution and the possibility of living in emotional peace with each other.

This may sound as if you, the caregiver, have to make all the compromises. To a certain extent, that is certainly true. Since the person with Alzheimer's cannot work from a fully functioning brain, the caregiver does indeed have to find solutions. If that seems unfair, remember that it is also very hard work to be the one who has Alzheimer's. It is frightening, lonely, and frustrating for the sufferer. Out of that comes most of the angers, tears, and difficult behaviors that you have to deal with. As a caregiver, you will find many solutions once you understand a behavior.

Be honest about who has the problem. Many problem behaviors are a problem to the caregiver. They do not cause any embarrassment, inconvenience, or risk to the person with Alzheimer's. Be clear about this. It will help you find solutions that work for you without causing conflict with the Alzheimer's sufferer.

For example, if the problem is someone undressing inappropriately indoors, you could close the curtains rather than fight about getting dressed again. This may not be the answer you wanted, but it may be the best workable solution. The fact that the behavior is a problem for you, and not for the person you care for does not make it *not* worth solving. As the caregiver, you must try to make life as pleasant for yourself as you can.

It can be hard enough looking after someone with Alzheimer's. You do not have to accept the unacceptable. You just have to be clear about the reality of the situation and the nature of the problem.

The rest of this chapter is arranged alphabetically by problem.

DAILY PROBLEM-SOLVING

Abuse

The old woman was sitting on a hospital gurney, waiting to be seen by the duty doctor. Her face was swollen and she had two black eyes. An X-ray technician stopped beside her.

"Oh my, what happened to you? Did you fall over?"

The old woman smiled and said cheerfully, "Oh no!"

"But your eyes are black and blue!" exclaimed the technician.

"Oh, well," said the old woman vaguely, "I suppose someone must have painted them."

That is an excellent example of why people with Alzheimer's are in special need of protection from abuse. They may have no memory of abuse. They cannot communicate clearly, and not everyone has the patience to decode what they say.

Abuse of the elderly is as unadmitted now as abuse of children used to be. Alzheimer's Association statistics say that up to 4 percent of the elderly are being abused. If 4 million Americans have Alzheimer's disease, that means some 160,000 elders with Alzheimer's are being abused. Unfortunately, abuse and Alzheimer's disease do go together.

It can be a very stressful disease for caregivers to cope with. This can bring out the kinds of feelings that lead to abuse. Abuse can occur in a number of ways—physical, emotional, sexual, and financial, as well as abuse through neglect and illegal restraint. The person with Alzheimer's is particularly helpless against abuse.

Caregivers have a moral ,as well as a legal, duty to protect anyone who is helpless to assert personal rights. If you suspect that family abuse of any kind is going on, you must contact your local elder abuse agency. Medical and social work professionals are also required to report abuse so that intervention can help everyone concerned. Nurses and doctors are also required to make abuse reports when marks of violence are found on their patients.

Every Area Agency on Aging in the country now has an elder abuse hotline listed in its resources, and doctors and emergency room personnel are being trained to look for signs of abuse. They are the same signs in elders as in children—bruises, falls, broken bones, none of which can be clearly accounted for. Even the suspicion of abuse can now lead to reports being made to senior and disabled services agencies for further investigation. It is an issue just beginning to surface.

One of the more dramatic stories to emerge that basically qualifies as abuse was the story of an Oregonian woman who was charged with abandoning her elderly father who had Alzheimer's disease. She took him out of state and left him in his wheelchair at a racetrack on the other side of the country, with a note falsifying his name. He was recognized in the newspapers by the staff of the care home where he had been residing. Although more dramatic than most, it was a story that typified the many issues usually concerned in abuse.

The daughter had been long estranged from her father and had personal and emotional problems that led to the action of abandonment. She said that her alcoholic father had sexually and physically abused her when she was young. The fact that she was placed on probation indicates that the court was aware of the complexity of the issues involved. Such problems seldom come about because an abuser is just plain cruel or thoughtless.

It is usually a combination of factors that causes people to injure those who need their help and protection. Overwhelming situations combined with personal inadequacies are the usual components. Most medical personnel and social workers can well understand the pressures that can lead to abuse. Their concern is to help the family cope. If you know that you are being abusive, or in danger of becoming so, get help immediately from your local senior services agency.

It is natural to sometimes feel angry at someone you are always looking after. However, it is entirely wrong to hit, push, or physically punish that person. It is normal to feel like yelling sometimes, but you have to find ways to express those impulses without being abusive to the person in your charge. For example, you could go for a ride in your car, wind up the windows, and yell as you drive. You might feel strange about that, but better out than in when it comes to emotional pressure.

Once your angry feelings start taking over, abuse may easily escalate, so get help before that. Get counseling, ask for help from any local office concerned with care for the elderly, go to support groups, and learn to laugh instead of getting mad.

Of course, not all abuse is physical or emotional. In Alzheimer's, it is not unusual for financial abuse to occur, with a family member or even an outside caregiver taking financial advantage of the incompetent person. This must also be reported by anyone who suspects it, and action can be taken by the justice system and by the social services system to safeguard the assets of an incompetent person.

Rarely can a demented person accurately identify being abused. However, it is fairly common for someone with Alzheimer's to claim that he or she is being abused when it is not true. People may accuse others of stealing from them when it is entirely untrue. This obviously complicates the issues.

Concerned people should keep an eye open for physical evidence that may suggest abuse, while also staying aware of the fact that any of these can result from legitimate accidents. If a caregiver is wrongly accused of abuse, this is a devastating event which will often result in someone giving up caring for that person.

Sam and his wife Marge took care of Sam's mother, who had Alzheimer's. They took her for an Alzheimer's work-up and then found themselves being reported to the local senior services agency for abuse when bruise marks were found on her arm. They had never abused her. She was prone to easy bruising, as many older people are, and had probably acquired the marks when being helped up from the low armchair she liked to sit in. The accusations shattered the couple and, soon after, they placed Sam's mother in a care home.

This sad story highlights the complexity of the abuse issue—one where we cannot exaggerate the dangers enough and yet must always be aware of witch-hunts.

Agitation

Many people with Alzheimer's have periods of agitation when they become anxious, worried, obsessive, fearful, or angry to a considerable degree. It is common for this to occur in the late afternoon, typically between 3 P.M. and 7 P.M.

This phenomenon is not peculiar to Alzheimer's disease. It is associated with many dementias and can also happen to older people who otherwise seem to be in good health. These late-afternoon periods of emotional agitation are often referred to as sun downing, since their timing seems to coincide with the setting of the sun. Although rare, it is not unknown for people to become agitated at other times of day on a regular basis. At mid-day or in the morning.

There have been many suggestions as to why this occurs. It may well be much more widespread than we think, since mothers of young children often have similar problems with fractious babies and infants during this same time period. People suffering a loss or depression also often report feeling worse at this time of day. Theorists guess that the agitation might be caused by a biochemical response to the fading of daylight. What really matters, however, is not the specific cause— since that cannot be clearly established at this point—but what you can do about it.

There are a number of different ways to help someone during this periodic agitation. Even if the agitation is caused by subtle biochemical changes in the body, there are still many ways to help alleviate the person's feelings.

When someone shows agitation, we can reasonably guess that fear and insecurity are the two prime feelings being expressed. What the person says at this time is not necessarily the actual cause of agitation. This is often when people refer to the themes that obsess them, commonly about one of their primary relationships—their parents, their spouse, or some other major figure in their life, often expressing a sense of loss or anger or anxiety.

"I'm waiting for my mother and my father," says the 88t-year-old.

"I want to go home now," says the woman standing in her own home.

Many caregivers more or less ignore such remarks— "Oh, she's just playing that same old tape again!"—but these themes are actually a very important part of the individual's resolution. They often underlie repetitive questions and demands (see "Repetitive Questions"). Wise caregivers find ways to help resolve the issues if possible, since they represent the underlying anxieties that trouble the person with Alzheimer's. It is helpful to listen responsively and offer emotional support.

In this way, emotional growth and resolution are made possible, even with the memory failure and cognitive limitations typical of Alzheimer's. The resolution comes with the acceptance of unconditional love, and this is certainly the basic relationship of caregiving. The life of the heart does not cease just because the brain is afflicted. In fact, the right hemisphere of the brain in which emotions live is often less damaged.

However unsatisfactory other primary relationships have been in a person's life, emotional fulfillment can come, with the help of the caregiver.

These themes which emerge in periods of sun downing should therefore be acknowledged. However, it will not be productive to concentrate on them during the time of agitation. Rational explanations do not dispel agitation. Telling an 88-year-old who wants her parents that her parents are dead is not useful, nor is it kind. It does not take care of her longing to be cared for as a loving parent cares for a child. It would be kinder to answer, "You really miss your family now, don't you?" or to ask, "Are you feeling lonely?"

It is more productive to deal with the probable underlying reasons for the agitation. A multipurpose approach is often successful. The likely factors in agitation are:

- tiredness
- hunger
- boredom
- emotional distress due to the day's events
- loneliness
- grief from the losses of old age
- fear caused by awareness that all is not well within
- feeling useless and unwanted.

Many people, old and young alike, suffer an energy drop in the late afternoon. Since people with Alzheimer's often need some activities to occupy them, it is easy to forget that they may also be exhausted by them. Plus, scientific studies show that the brain of a person with Alzheimer's is in constant action, presumably trying to get round the roadblocks to thinking.

Since these are old people with a serious debilitating illness, we need to remember that the illness also makes it impossible for them to recognize or articulate their exhaustion. Therefore, the caregiver must be aware of that possibility. When late-afternoon agitation is a regular event, try several of the following:

• Add an after-lunch nap to the routine. This can also be a welcome opportunity for the caregiver to rest too, perhaps even curling up in the same bed or on the same comfortable sofa;

• If this is not acceptable, try extending morning sleeping hours by encouraging the person to stay in bed longer;

• Offer an energy snack of some kind in mid-afternoon to help avoid this energy drop, such as fruit and yogurt, fruit juice, or a piece of cake with tea or coffee;

• Give strong emotional support at this time, perhaps by playing a beloved piece of music and sitting with your arm around the person while you both listen together;

• Distract the person from agitation by producing entertainment. Some people enjoy particular videos and will happily watch the same one day after day.

Others enjoy the comedy or discussion programs on television in late afternoon. Even if they do not follow them entirely in a cognitive sense, the social energy of these programs is pleasantly entertaining for some impaired people.

• Take a walk together, or go for a drive to someplace where you can sit and enjoy what ever's going on.

Times of agitation, paradoxically enough, can also be times of great emotional clarity. This may well be the time at which the person with Alzheimer's feels most aware of personal losses. If this is so, do not try to make things right with false consolation. When we deny someone the chance to express pain and fear, we force the person into terrible loneliness.

Do not be afraid to acknowledge the illness and the impairment. You can absolutely assume that it has been noticed! Say something like, "Yes, I know it's hard now that you can't do things like you used to. It's awful to keep forgetting things."

You might add reassuringly, "You know, it's not your fault. You have a physical illness that makes you forget things. A lot of other people have this illness too. It's just one of those hard things that happens sometimes. I'm sorry."

Since memory impairment is a major feature of this illness, you may have to remind the person of this whenever it seems appropriate. Do not be afraid to tell a person he or she has an illness that causes forgetfulness. You will be surprised how often it cheers a person up to hear about that illness.

Most people with Alzheimer's disease forget they have the disease and therefore blame themselves for being stupid or fear that they are going mad. It is quite a relief to know that there is a reason for what is happening. Be sure to show a lot of affection when these discussions are going on, to reinforce the message that the person is loved exactly as he or she is right now.

Caregivers who try this multi-faceted approach report finding it successful, so much so that in a number of cases the periods of agitation have actually ceased to occur on a regular basis.

Remember that agitation can be catching. Do not allow yourself to be infected by it. Stay calm within, knowing that it will pass. Speak quietly and kindly to the one who is agitated. Remember that you do not have a duty to take the agitation away. It is only a passing mood and it does no real harm. It will, like most other things, be forgotten. This is the blessing of Alzheimer's disease, as well as its curse.

It is very important that you do not insist on drugging agitation out of people as a first resort. Some family members over-react to a parent's agitation and want to suppress it, really because of their own inner issues and emotional health. Because you get upset is absolutely not a reason to drug another person, especially an elder with dementia whose fragile health often cannot support strong medication. That comment does not apply to abnormally extended periods of agitation. If someone is frantic or raging all night long, you must obtain a psychiatric work-up for that person. That is not normal sun downing.

Apart from sun downing, most other episodes of agitation are reactive. They happen in response to something in the environment—an event, a person, a surprise, a loss, a change. These can be classified as "catastrophic reactions" Look ahead for that section.

Alcohol

Some of the problems of Alzheimer's may be exaggerated through overuse of alcohol. The problem behaviors typical of the heavy drinker do not disappear when Alzheimer's takes over. Early Alzheimer symptoms are often masked by or mistaken for alcoholism, especially if the person is self-medicating the emotional pain by drinking. When Rita Hayworth was beginning to manifest Alzheimer's disease, people assumed that she was an alcoholic.

Once the disease has been diagnosed, unfortunately, the patterns of destructive and difficult behavior associated with heavy alcohol use may be likely to remain and are increased by the progress of Alzheimer's disease. It is not an enviable task to be a caregiver to a heavy drinker who also has Alzheimer's. There can be added problems in that lifelong abuse of alcohol can also lead to dementia in itself, although not to Alzheimer's disease.

The most important thing is at least to reduce the amount of alcohol the person drinks. As the Alzheimer's progresses, the person will be less and less able to manage to buy alcohol, and the caregiver should not supply it.

In cases of mild drinking, there may be no reason why a person should not continue unless the alcohol presents a dangerous combination with prescribed medications. Medical advice should be sought. In the case of a couple who have always indulged in heavy drinking together, there is the question of whether continuing this pattern is actually an abuse of the partner with Alzheimer's.

Many caregivers observe that the confusion typical of Alzheimer's may be increased when alcohol is consumed, as can the aggressive behavior. If, as a caregiver, you are going to allow the person with Alzheimer's to drink alcohol, you must observe what effect it has and act cautiously on behalf of the person who is impaired.

Anger

First, take an honest look at any anger issues you may have around being a caregiver. If you have continuous responsibility for a person with Alzheimer's, you probably get very tired, lonely and fed-up from time to time, and under such circumstances small irritations can lead to feeling a great deal of anger. If you have a close relative or partner with Alzheimer's, you may have feelings of anger that are really connected with your sense of loss.

It is natural to feel angry that you have to take complete care of someone who used to be a partner but no longer can fulfill the balancing role you once appreciated. It is natural to feel angry that you have to take care of this woman who used to be your mother and now is more like your own child.

Not everyone feels angry about such things, but probably most people do at one time or another. If you never feel angry, perhaps you feel guilty. It might be worth taking a closer look at your emotions if you often feel guilty. Psychologists consider that guilt often masks unacceptable feelings of anger. Other feelings of anger can also underlie changes in relationships. If, for example, you now have to take care of your mother as if she were your child, when she never really fulfilled your own longing for love when you were little, you are likely to feel very angry. It is hard to give another person the kind of love you never received.

If someone you once admired now behaves in ways that frighten or disgust you because of this illness, you may well feel angry. If you feel overworked, unappreciated, and lonely, and never get enough sleep, there is a good chance you also get angry pretty often. It is common for caregivers to feel angry occasionally, often, or even all the time. It is not wrong. A feeling just is.

Unfortunately, anger reduces your ability to be a good care- giver. It is also hard work. It uses up energy you need for other things, like enjoying life. It reduces your ability to feel compassion. It makes you feel guilty too and it takes away your sense of humor altogether. Therefore, you do need to help yourself if you often feel angry. Otherwise, harmful stress will build up to make you feel bad and increase the risk of abuse.

One way to start helping yourself is to become clear about what exactly is making you feel angry. You can even sit down and make a list of all the reasons.

That will help you to see what is involved, since there are often multiple factors.

Your first duty is to take care of yourself properly. That includes taking time off, getting enough sleep, finding ways to relax, and getting professional help when it is needed. It is not good enough to say you cannot get help. Usually when people say they cannot get help, what they really mean is that they have not asked. Often this is false pride. Dealing with Alzheimer's is very exhausting and no one can deal with it alone for long without paying a terrible price. It does take some trouble on your part to find the right help, but you must do it and it is really worth the effort.

If you know your anger comes out of stress, you must find relief. In many communities, there are Alzheimer day-care or respite centers to which you can take your person with Alzheimer's and get at least a morning or afternoon off for yourself (see "Day Centers" in chapter 9). Never assume that your charge could not or would not adapt to being in such a setting. Actually, day-activity centers can be more entertaining and supportive than home life, and they add some appropriate stimulus to a somewhat empty life. Most people do enjoy them, just as most little children eventually enjoy kindergarten or preschool after some tears. Be prepared to ask friends, relatives, or even members of your church or some similar organization to help with an occasional afternoon duty.

Often, the reason people do not offer to help is that they are discouraged by the caregiver—"Oh, no, we're fine!"—or because they simply do not know what they could do. Be really specific about what people can do for you.

Ask, "Would you take Mother for a half-hour drive one afternoon next week?" or "Would you sit with George for a couple of hours while I take time off? He likes to be read to."

Most people are afraid of helping only because they are nervous that they will inadvertently do something harmful or hurtful. They just need a little practice and some advice from you. Join an Alzheimer's support group and start to trade some care with others in the same position. Get counseling if you want help with your inner feelings. Read self-help books and follow the suggestions in them.

All this advice comes in the anger section here for good reason. This is part of looking after yourself so that stress does not make you constantly angry. Another benefit of a support group is that it provides a place where you can safely talk about your feelings and the stresses of caregiving. Do not unload too much on your friends or you might wear them out. Alzheimer's is uniquely taxing in that the caregiver not only has full responsibility for the physical care of another person, but also has to act as the full-time interpreter of the world around to the person who has the illness. The world of Alzheimer's makes very little sense, and it is the caregiver who must find ways to explain, to link, to fill out the missing pieces, and then to supply the emotional support and understanding that is needed.

Add to this the fact that many people with Alzheimer's are physically fit and bursting with energy, and the task really becomes taxing.

This is why you need to be among those who understand what you are up against. If you know your anger does not arise only from present circumstances but is rooted in the past, then find someone who will help you work through that old unexpressed rage. If you do not, it will emerge inappropriately. Even if your anger comes from your parent not having taken care of you enough when you were a child, it is useless to take that anger out on the parent who is now too sick to understand or just does not remember any more. It is not fair and, more importantly, it does not help you.

You need to be able to talk over those old unresolved issues with someone who can help you—a therapist, a counselor, a minister, an old friend, a new friend. If you need to talk to someone in a hurry, call a suicide hotline, where you can talk anonymously if you want to. You do not have to be actually suicidal to call. The Alzheimer's Association also has a national hotline and experts who understand your situation.

So much for your anger as a caregiver. Now to the anger of the person with Alzheimer's disease. You hear a lot about it, so much so that you might think everyone who has Alzheimer's also has tremendous attacks of rage. That is not true. Some people never become angry, while others are only occasionally or temporarily angry. This tends to happen in the earlier stages of the disease, when people become aware of their losses and become frightened. Some people do become violent later, but this is often in reaction to what is happening around them, as well as to them. Often they can be helped by family members being prepared to talk about the reality of their situation.

All too often, family members decide not to mention the illness, thus condemning the sick person to terrible loneliness.

"I couldn't tell my husband he has Alzheimer's," says Millie, "it would just upset him so much."

There are still many instances of denial, where neither the person with the illness nor family members speak about Alzheimer's. Relatives withhold the truth of diagnosis, mistakenly feeling that this spares the person worry. In fact, nothing is more worrying than wondering what is wrong and why it is steadily getting worse. No one with Alzheimer's disease is unaware of it, whether the name is ever spoken or not.

Many people, on the other hand, never seem to experience rage, so do not worry about it. The most important thing to understand is that all anger is based on something that is real to the person with Alzheimer's. The anger is largely reactive, and the caregiver's task is to figure out what the person is reacting to. Sometimes, sadly, it is anger that has been stifled over the years and that begins to emerge because the person's inhibitions are now reduced. These are the people you sometimes hear about, like the mild-mannered man who becomes a raging tyrant. Reports from people working in the field suggest that these people were often angry before but had kept it within. With the encroachment of the disease, they could not stifle their feelings any more.

Typical of this was the long-suffering, self-effacing wife of a powerful business magnate.

She became a creature possessed as she plainly showed the early signs of Alzheimer's disease. Her family referred to these episodes as "Mother's nerves," whereas in fact it was her rage at being emotionally neglected for years by her husband who was hard, intolerant, and inattentive. As her illness progressed, it became more and more apparent that she had been deeply unhappy for years.

Such stories are common but they are not really the typical rages of Alzheimer's, which tend to be fierce and short. When dealing with these rages, it is always best to begin by acknowledging the anger. You can usually guess what triggered the anger and can then respond with empathy.

"I know it must be so frustrating when you can't find the words."

"It's infuriating to have to struggle with your clothes like that, isn't it?"

"It really makes me mad too when I get things mixed up."

These comments help by showing that you understand. Sometimes, however, it might be best simply to let the person express the anger. You can make appropriate comments in a calm, soothing voice. That shows you care, that you can accept the anger, that emotional reassurance is there. There are a variety of other ways to deal with rage. You can use distraction, redirection into a new activity or taking the person into another room or out of the house altogether.

Car rides can be a very useful way to soothe angry or distressed feelings. Being in a car is safe and cozy and entertaining without being demanding.

It can be effective to ignore your person's anger. This can be done either while remaining in the room where your person is or by leaving the room. If you do leave the

147

room—and this can be useful in giving the person the literal space in which to spill out emotions—make it clear why you are leaving and that your absence is not punitive.

"I'm going next door for a few minutes now. When you feel ready, I'll be back."

This gives the person privacy for the feelings that need to come out. It also gives you the space in which to gather yourself together. Alzheimer anger can be very invasive, since the person often cannot identify its true origin and therefore may blame the caregiver.

"You don't give a damn about me" shouts the woman who really is trying to express her loneliness and fear within the impairing illness that is making her unfamiliar even to herself.

In all circumstances, the first responsibility of the caregiver is to ensure that no harm befalls the person with Alzheimer's. The second is to try not to take the outburst personally, even if personal remarks are made. It is entirely fitting that someone suffering the great losses and limitations of the disease feels angry. Family members may find themselves the target of this anger—accusations of theft, abandonment, hostility, not caring—simply because they are the closest to the person with Alzheimer's. It is only with them that the person can express the real fear and terror that lies within.

This does not usually feel like a privilege to caring family members, but in a way it is a compliment. Anger can simply be part of the process of working through acceptance of the illness. As such, family members should try to accept it. However, under no circumstances should the caregiver ever allow physical abuse to happen. Caregivers who firmly state that certain behavior is unacceptable report that the behavior often does in fact cease or become modified so that it is no longer a physical threat.

If you cannot stop the abuse, however, you may have to resort to getting help. Call the police if you feel in danger of being injured by someone you cannot control. Ask your doctor for help with medication if long-term chemical control is needed, but be honest about carefully examining your own interactions and support of the person before calling for medication.

The reality is that on-going violence is not common in Alzheimer's. It usually indicates the presence of mental health issues which need skilled diagnosis and a care regime. Sadly, much so-called Alzheimer's diagnosis may totally overlook these issues. Most people with Alzheimer's see a neurologist for final diagnosis, not a psychiatrist. This can mean a family is left to deal with a situation that is not actually Alzheimer's or may be both dementia plus a mental health condition. Do not hesitate to get further diagnosis, by getting a referral to a psychiatrist. The cost is covered by Medicare or insurance and it could make all the difference to health, safety and family caregiving.

Behavior Problems
This category covers any behavior that is inappropriate to the occasion. This includes a wide range of possibilities, from taking out false teeth in public and washing them in a coffee cup to feeding cat food to the squirrels. People with Alzheimer's do strange things simply because their cognitive powers have been affected and they may no longer remember what is appropriate on all occasions.

Nearly all our social behavior is learned, and therefore it can be unlearned in the course of a brain-impairing disease. The best way to cope with odd behavior in someone with Alzheimer's is to show the same humor, understanding, and kindness you would with a child. Do not ask why the person did such a thing.

Obviously it was done because social appropriateness has been eroded as a concept. Instead, merely indicate in a nonjudgmental manner what you would like the person to do,

"It probably isn't such a good idea to wash your teeth in your coffee. Maybe you could pop them back into your mouth now."

If you feel embarrassed, count to ten and calm yourself may before speaking. If you become agitated, so too will the person with Alzheimer's. Strangers are often much kinder and more tolerant than you might fear in your embarrassment. Assume the best. If you feel you must do something to warn others, you could follow the example of one man whose wife had an unusual problem with excess saliva.

While walking through a very high-class department store, she spat on a bunch of silk flowers. He apologized and spoke with dignity,.

"My wife isn't well and I'd be glad to pay for those." He was not charged for them.

Another man reports that his wife tended to buttonhole strangers and, like the Ancient Mariner, subject them to long, rambling monologues. He handed them a small card on which was written, "My wife has Alzheimer's disease" to alert them to the basic situation. Almost invariably, people would listen politely to her for a while and then gracefully extract themselves as soon as they reasonably could. People often appreciate opportunities to be compassionate and kind.

If others do react badly, remember it is their own fear breaking out. Try to forgive them. They are probably terrified that one day they too might have Alzheimer's disease.

Catastrophic Reactions

This means overreaction to an event or stimulus, in the form of anger, fear, anxiety grief, or some other powerful emotion. It usually happens because the person does not understand what is going on or because he or she experiences a strong emotional feeling about some event.

An 85-year-old woman may weep on hearing that her parents are dead, although they have been dead for many years. Because of her memory loss , she had forgotten this and the news comes afresh to her. A man may become terrified while standing under the shower because he no longer expects water will come rushing out of it.

The sudden event frightens him. He does not understand what is going on, why the water is pouring out, what he should do about it. In other situations, overreaction may arise from the way in which the person with Alzheimer's interprets a situation.

"I haven't stolen anything. I'm not a thief!" shouts Ruth, entirely out of the blue. Ruth may have been dreaming, or she may have been stirred by a memory, or she may have misheard and misinterpreted something said by another person. She needs to be soothed, comforted, and then, as soon as it seems appropriate, distracted by some other activity.

Sometimes Carlos weeps and berates himself, crying, "I'm useless. I might as well be dead. I'm so stupid!" This tends to happen after he has failed to carry out some task or feels belittled or abandoned.

Other catastrophic reactions may be brought about by caregivers intervening too roughly or too quickly. Never confront, always persuade. Never give orders, always make suggestions. Never push or pull roughly, always guide gently. If you show violence, you will receive violence. You can avoid catastrophic reactions by giving plenty of time for preparations and departures, gently explaining what is going on in a simple way, and never trying to force the situation.

When you try to force someone with Alzheimer's to do something, you are treating that person as an object, not as a human being. You are likely to be taught an unpleasant lesson in return.

Use your imagination compassionately and you will usually understand the basis of a catastrophic reaction. The best way to deal with it is, if possible, to remove the cause. In any case, remain calm, reassuring, and patient. Do not become angry or agitated, since this only makes things worse. Such reactions are soon over and forgotten. Although they are emotionally powerful at the time, they are not really very significant.

Confrontation

Never waste your energy by trying to confront people with Alzheimer's disease. You will only bring about a catastrophic reaction. If you are trying to prove them wrong through rational explanation, they will react badly because they have an impaired ability to follow rational thought. So they feel trapped and attacked.

They know their feelings and you cannot argue them out of their feelings. An 88-year-old woman in an Alzheimer's care unit insisted she had to go home to feed her two little boys since they would be home from school. The duty nurse patiently explained that her two little boys were now in their sixties and obviously did not need her to cook their dinners after school. She followed the whole explanation carefully and then said, looking directly at the nurse, "I know what you told me and even if it's true, I can only tell you that in here there are two little boys that need me," patting her heart as she spoke.

Trying to logically prove someone with Alzheimer's wrong only causes frustration and perhaps rage, often for both parties.

Trying to make your person do something, you will be met by resistance against the pressure you are creating. If you are in a hurry, the person will slow down or even have an accident of incontinence. If you are trying to make the person admit to being impaired, natural resentment will follow.

As in any good people management, the tools to use are persuasion, kindness, and incentive. If you are being confrontational, ask yourself why. The chances are that you are feeling angry and not really admitting it. Deal with your own anger without trying to make the person with Alzheimer's wrong.

Dehydration

This is a frequent problem among all older people and merits special attention since it causes particular problems in Alzheimer's. Some experts think the thirst mechanism becomes deficient in old age, while others suggest that medications may be responsible. Whatever the cause, dehydration is common. Older people simply do not drink enough water and do not feel thirsty. Additionally, many older people were never in the habit of drinking water and often dislike it.

For the general maintenance of good hydration, at least four large glasses of water a day are required, and some experts suggest that this figure should be even more This is apart from tea, coffee, alcohol, soft drinks, or milk. It is especially important to make sure that people with Alzheimer's consume sufficient fluids, since they are unlikely to express a wish for drinks on their own initiative.

If they are reluctant to drink large amounts of water, give it to them in little glasses on a regular basis. One or two small glasses per hour throughout the day will ensure they get all the water they need. If they do not like water, add a touch of fruit juice or squeeze some lemon into the water. Try an herbal tea without any caffeine in it, either hot or cold, as another way of getting fluid into them. If the person is reluctant to drink, say "The doctor says you must." That often works.

Confusion increases in people who are dehydrated, so always get fluids into someone who seems to be particularly confused for no known reason. Likewise, give a drink of water at periods of agitation. There is a quick-check test for dehydration. Pinch the person's skin. The hand is a good place to do this, but ask permission first, of course. If the skin takes a long time to settle into place, that person is dehydrated. Another clue is constipation. Despite everything that has been claimed for fiber in the diet, the main reason why people are constipated is that they do not drink enough water.

Depression

Depression can be a problem both for the caregiver and for the person with Alzheimer's, for obvious reasons. Both face considerable displacement of their previous lives, both may well be feeling lonely and frightened, and both may also be hiding considerable feelings of anger. Depression, as well as being an emotional expression of hopelessness and despair, often conceals anger.

James had been taken, against his will, to a nursing home. He sat in a chair with his face in his lap much of the day, or he covered his face with a scarf. When people asked him why he was doing it, he said, "I wish I were dead. I can't stand this."

The visiting psychiatrist decided to put James on antidepressants but, before it could be done, James had managed to die. James's reaction was emotionally valid. He did not want to be there. He was by nature a solitary, unsociable person who only wanted to be left alone. Much depression among older people is valid, in that it reflects real sorrow and grief at losses.

This grief is often hard for caregivers to bear, both at home and in nursing facilities. They tend to want to fix the grief with mood-control medication. Before turning to medications, which might have undesirable side effects, it would often be much more humane to try to identify and work with the causes of depression. Or to support the grieving by being there as a validating presence, "I know, I understand, of course you feel unhappy."

Causes of Depression:
- reaction to the losses caused by the illness;
- loneliness;
- boredom and lack of interests;
- lack of self-esteem;
- other losses and stresses in life, such as the loss of a partner or withdrawal of children from a parent's life;
- loss of friendship or longterm lack of friendships;
- underlying feelings of conflict, such as anger or fear.

It does not necessarily take a therapist to work some of these things out. A sensitive caregiver is open to dealing with them and often talking about them is the only action needed. It is important to look for openings given by the person with Alzheimer's. These might include any of the following.
- "Oh, what's the point anyway?"
- "Why should I be bothered?"
- "I might as well be dead."
- "Everybody hates me."

Remarks like these tell you how bad the person is feeling. Allow free expression of feeling and be accepting. Do not deny the feelings. Do not try to fix them, since you cannot. Show whose side you are on. When trust has been established between you, try to work on those feelings by talking more about them.

Listen carefully, since communication is so hard for the person with Alzheimer's. Never tell someone who is depressed to cheer up or try to change feelings by arguing about them. This approach attacks the person's integrity and denies what is felt to be true. It makes a person feel even more lonely.

Do not offer treats as bribes to force someone to feel better—it does not work. Encourage the person to talk about what is within. Even a badly-impaired person can nevertheless have a sense of inner feelings and want to express them and get support for them. As a caregiver, never fall into the trap of dismissing depression as part of the illness. The person with Alzheimer's has good reason to be depressed but, on the other hand, many people with Alzheimer's are habitually cheerful and upbeat.

One health professional tried the following exercise with a group of women with Alzheimer's, all of whom looked especially depressed one morning. She got them to stand up and shout, "I feel sad!"

They started slowly, not very willingly, but they followed her example. Soon they were shouting with great gusto, "I feel sad," at which point she changed their chorus to "I feel mad!"

Once they had shouted that a few times, they had cheered up considerably. The exercise works well even with one person. Encourage an emphatic up-and-down arm movement to accompany the chant. If you are a caregiver to someone who seems very depressed, it's useful to talk to the person's doctor to find out if any of the medications the person is taking could be contributing to the depression.

This is not unusual among older people in general. Many heart medications cause depression. Medication-caused depression is a particular danger among people with Alzheimer's because their physiological reactions to medications may be different.

If you are satisfied that medication is not the cause of depression and you are genuinely anxious about the person's state of mind, it may be time to talk to your doctor about the possibility of antidepressants. Before you do that, however, you should be aware of two things. One is that you must have a doctor who is both interested and informed about Alzheimer's disease. The second is that few medications that alter states of mind do so without adversely affecting the patient in several other ways. As a caregiver, you must get full information on any anticipated adverse effects, and you must also become very observant so that you can quickly become aware of changes due to medication and follow up with further medical consultations.

Doctors

It may seem unfair to list doctors under problems, but it is just a reminder that as a caregiver you need access to a really good doctor. A good doctor for someone with Alzheimer's is someone who knows a lot about Alzheimer's and learns more all the time. A good doctor does not treat an old person as if illness is supposed to be the expected lot of old age. A good doctor does not attribute every health problem in a person with Alzheimer's to the disease itself. Conversely, a good doctor knows that normal symptoms of ill health can be distorted or utterly changed in a person with Alzheimer's and acts with appropriate caution.

A good doctor will treat the Alzheimer's patient with respect. That means asking the patient directly the questions that may afterward have to be addressed to the caregiver. It means acknowledging the problems a caregiver may have in administering medicine and trying to help the caregiver find innovative solutions. It should also mean that medical appointments are kept promptly by the doctor so that the person with Alzheimer's is not subject to the tensions of waiting.

If you are not satisfied with your doctor, get another one. There are plenty of doctors out there and you plenty for them, so shop around just as you would with any other high-cost investment. Choose the one who meets your needs and the needs of the person with Alzheimer's best.

Good doctors do not resent time spent in communication and are willing to explain medical facts and prescriptions in language that normal people use. They do not use vague and meaningless phrases like, "She's a bit senile," or "Well, what can you expect at his age?"

They behave as if Alzheimer's is the debilitating and challenging disease that it really is for both sufferers and caregivers.

Driving

My opinion is that people who have been diagnosed as having Alzheimer's disease should NOT be driving.

Opinions do vary on this and even official rulings vary. Some states require doctors to report patients they have diagnosed as having the disease to the relevant Department of Motor Vehicles so that they can be retested. Others do not require this.

Even within the world of Alzheimer's, experts disagree. They differ because they feel that patients differ. One person with Alzheimer's may still show excellent driving judgment, another may be very poorly coordinated. In our society, driving is an important mark of freedom. It is often the biggest factor in keeping a sense of independence. To lose the car is to lose some ability to manage life.

Recent research reveals that three out of ten people diagnosed with Alzheimer's had been involved in a serious car accident in the previous few months. Three more had small accidents. Furthermore, one in ten were said by caregivers to have caused an accident. These are chilling statistics—chilling enough to suggest that no one with Alzheimer's should be driving.

It is hard to lose access to a car when that is what one has been used to. However, it is undoubtedly also true that having Alzheimer's can and does affect judgment in too many ways to maintain safe driving. It not only affects memory, so that people may drive erratically while trying to work out where they are going; it also affects judgment, vision, and the awareness of what proper driving actually is.

Someone with Alzheimer's may drive onto the freeway using the wrong ramp. This has happened more than once, resulting in death for one or more parties.

Others with Alzheimer's have driven on the sidewalk or right into buildings. Of the drivers cited to be reviewed for competency by the California DMV, 50 percent have lost their licenses. As a society, we have to consider the right of everyone to be safe, not just the right of a person with Alzheimer's to maintain personal freedom. Family members often report their own terror at the driving capacity of the person who has Alzheimer's, but at the same time do not want that person to be without transportation.

Sometimes a spouse can take over the driving, simply by stating firmly that her husband's driving now worries her. Sometimes families can get their doctor to explain to the patient that driving is no longer possible. One family reports that their doctor told his patient, "Joe, if you won't stop driving your car, I'm not going to see you any more."

In Joe's case, it worked and his wife took over the driving. In other families, the decision to stop someone driving comes very hard. One son actually took his father's car keys and sold the car. His father then bought himself a new vehicle, leaving his son to do the same thing again. It is a problem with no easy solution.

Eventually, everyone who has Alzheimer's reaches a point where driving is no longer possible. Sometimes people voluntarily retire from driving at this point. In other cases, their family members have to fight them. It often seems to be harder for men to give up their right to drive than for women. Unfortunately, their families sometimes see it only as a matter between family members, forgetting the danger to others. The question of driving or not driving often has more to do with family relationships.

Family dynamics—the man whose wife cannot oppose him, the mother whose children want to indulge her—often prolong the issue well into the anger zone of potentially fatal accidents. The dynamics have to be dealt with by the family, sometimes with help from a doctor, social worker, or other professional. The basic issue for the family members should be to keep everyone safe, both the person with Alzheimer's and the child walking across the road or the young man driving on the freeway. Any move to stop all driving should be allied with an alternative transportation plan, to be laid before the family member at the same time he or she is told that driving is no longer possible.

The real question to ask if you are confronted with this issue is, "How will I feel when someone dies because of this person driving, when I knew all along it was time to stop?"

That really is the bottom line on letting someone with Alzheimer's drive when impairment makes it no longer safe to do so. Another point well worth considering is that if someone with Alzheimer's has any trauma, such as a car accident, it invariably brings about a decline in general ability to manage and a further step-down in the course of the Alzheimer's. Therefore, it is not the kindness it may seem to be to let that person continue driving until the inevitable accident occurs.

Eating

Problems with eating can take a number of forms—eating too much, too little, too slowly, or too often.

Most people with Alzheimer's develop an intense hunger for sugar. Sugar imbalance may be part of the cause, as an "overdrive" in the system that demands constant calorific input, with sugar being the most popular item desired. Many caregivers have no problem monitoring sugar intake. Others find that their charges demand constant ice cream, cookies, and chocolate bars. One man reported that his wife would eat a whole carton of chocolate ice cream bars out of the freezer every day.

Certainly there is no point in expecting the person who is sick to regulate his or her demands for food, any more than you would let your three-year-old plan the daily menu. If you cannot hide extra food or cannot deny its existence, do not buy it in the first place. Limit its use to when you go out instead.

On the other hand, as concerned as many of us are about healthy diet these days, we need to ask ourselves what we are saving people for—so they can be physically healthy as their brain deteriorates? As long as someone is not grossly overweight or diabetic, tightly controlled diets are not as important as they once might have been. The typical picture of Alzheimer's is that people gain weight as they grow more ill, exercise less, and indulge their whims. Then they lose weight as the illness progresses. You must decide for yourself what your values are on this issue.

A number of people lose interest in food but will eat when it is set before them. We know that people with dementia usually lose their sense of smell. This means that food becomes tasteless to them. You might want to spice food up for them instead of keeping it bland.

"My mother has become very fussy about how her food looks. She wants each kind of food quite separate from the rest and she eats each item separately. First she'll eat all the peas, then all the meat, and so on," Manny said, puzzled. This is common, and presumably it has something to do with Alzheimer perceptions of food on the plate. Whatever it is, just humor these whims. Even if people say they do not want to eat, put food before them without comment. Often they will eat it once it is there. Do not ask what people want, but suggest something tactfully.

"I could make you a great omelet—you know how you always love that," is much more effective than, "What would you like for dinner?"

Visual-perceptual problems may develop that manifest in strange eating patterns. Hannah eats the whole of one side of her plate of food and then stops. Only if the caregiver turns the plate around will she then eat the other side. We must assume that brain damage may mean she actually sees only one side at a time or perhaps she has genuine sight issues.

Learn from all good mothers and do not make food a battleground. Eating issues will be abound if you do.

Anne always says, "I don't want to eat. I'm not hungry."

Then her daughter got into a fight with her every mealtime. After an Alzheimer's workshop, she learned to say instead, "Oh, well, I'll just leave it there in case."

Anne would eat it without fail.

If someone genuinely loses all interest in food, think about serving high-protein shakes instead. That will still supply everything the person needs. A shake does not have to include milk. You could use soy milk, fruit juice, ice cream, yogurt, or non- dairy creamers. Look on the internet for great recipes.

Forgetfulness

This, of course, is the essence of Alzheimer's disease, its main warning sign. Until we know someone who has severe memory problems, however, most of us cannot imagine how deeply it cuts through the fabric of life. Our lives as human beings depend upon the fact that our mind weaves together our past and our present to make our future. Once we cannot rely upon our minds to perform the weaving function, everything starts to come apart. Daily life unravels.

In Alzheimer's disease and other dementias, the short-term memory function is damaged first, followed by long-term memory issues, although many people retain some parts of long-term memory to a surprising degree, often matching that of elders with no dementia. Effectively, this means that at first the main problems are ones of forgetfulness in daily life, similar to those experienced occasionally by most people

Typically, the difference is that people with Alzheimer's may have less real awareness of their forgetting and things will not come back to them later, as happens to normal people. Eventually, they forget entire days.

As one woman wrote in her diary, several years before her diagnosis, "Strange, I do not remember at all what I did yesterday."

In this earlier stage, there is also an accompanying loss of cognitive ability, experienced by family members as a sense of something being not quite right, without them being able to put their fingers on it.

The pattern of forgetfulness varies, probably according to the person's former mind habits. This variation often deceives people at first into thinking that the person with Alzheimer's could remember if he or she chose to do so. Many people retain excellent long-term memory and can tell every detail of their childhood while not knowing who was sitting with them five minutes before. Memory ability can vary literally from day to day, according to how well the person is feeling.

The fact is that Alzheimer's has infinite variations. Mavis cannot remember how to get from one room to the next, but she can play an excellent game of bridge, remembering all the cards that have been played and making correct calls. Frank, who is not sure who his son is, can still play the piano beautifully. So we have to accept that memory goes but that its going produces highly individual behaviors. It will be apparent to the caregiver what parts of memory are missing and where support is needed. For a while, written notes can be useful reminders to many people. They work to keep some people functional for quite a long time.

It can also be useful to label drawers and cupboards to remind someone of where certain necessary things can be found. The most important thing is to realize that the decline in memory cannot be reversed or stopped by such reminders. Sometimes, caregivers label entire households from top to bottom in an effort to help the person with Alzheimer's. In fact, that is merely confusing. Caregivers must examine the true needs of the person with Alzheimer's and work within that limit. One example of good use of labeling was the family that put up the following labels in the kitchen. "Cheerios," "milk," and "cat food." Those labels reflected the most important daily needs of the person with Alzheimer's in that household.

Another good example was the blackboard on which one family wrote a list of each day's happenings.

Do not ever test the memory of a person with Alzheimer's. Do not ask, "Do you know who this is?" or "Do you remember me coming last week?" If the answer is no, it is distressing for both parties. Accept that the person probably cannot remember and there is nothing personal in it.

When memory goes, that can also mean we forget the year we are in. The ship of memory can anchor anywhere without us knowing the difference, if someone is living in the memory year of 1932, this is not craziness. It is the logical result of memory loss.

Hoarding

`Betty has twenty-two cans of blackberries stored in her cupboard. She bought them because she liked the picture on the label. Mabel has fifty-three tissues in her handbag. George hides his money. So far, several hundred

164

dollars have gone missing but no one knows where he has hidden them. Maria, who lives in a nursing home, has sixteen stuffed animals jammed into her bedside locker. She "collected" them from other residents' rooms.

Several varieties of hoarding are common to people with Alzheimer's. The most difficult is the hoarding or hiding of money. It is difficult because the money is effectively lost until it can be rediscovered by the caregiver and also because it can lead to accusations of stealing. Caregivers often mention that they or others are accused of stealing money. These accusations are sometimes classified medically as evidence of paranoia. However, this is really not evidence of paranoia, but the logical result of hiding money and having no memory of having done so. Naturally, under such conditions, it looks to the person with Alzheimer's as if someone else has taken the money.

As a caregiver, you will have to find some workable arrangement around hoarding. A hoarder will not be persuaded to stop hoarding, although this tendency may disappear later in the illness. Hoarding is a natural response to fear and insecurity. It is the way in which the person with Alzheimer's is trying to keep the universe under control, particularly in the areas that especially worry the individual. Some worry about money most, and so they will hide it from the potential thieves who are already apparently stealing it. Others worry about food and hide that away. Still others collect particular things that presumably represent security or pleasure to them.

None of us likes to be without money. It represents our independence and our power in the world. Therefore, a workable solution needs to be found that will allow the person to have some money without losing large sums. You might discuss the issue and find an acceptable sum that makes the person feel secure. One woman was content with a $5 bill being left in her purse each day. Another woman was given $300 twice a month. Another man had a pile of play money and did not know the difference. The arrangement will depend on how much the person needs and knows. It is important for you to accept that if a certain amount of money is going to be hoarded or simply disappear, then that is what will happen. Either the money will turn up later or it will not. In either case, an impaired person is still a human being with certain needs to have access to personal money, even if that allowance is small.

Keeping to the agreement may be hard. For one thing, the person will probably have forgotten that any such agreement has been made. One caregiver's solution was to make an agreement that both she and her charge then signed. In the future, when the woman asked where her money was, they would read over the agreement together, which stated that she would have access to $5 a day, and this usually mollified the woman.

Basically it is better not to argue too much over the issue but to deal with it by saying that no more money is available at that point for some reason. One woman always told her husband, "The bank is closed now, honey,"

Money arguments are about power and independence as much as they are about trust, so you may need to find other ways to enhance the individual's self hood. Most hoarding comes down to the understanding and acceptance of the caregiver, since hoarders are usually determined and cunning in their pursuit of control of an out-of-control world. Your sense of humor will go far to help you in this situation.

It is important to realize that the other side of hoarding is that the person with Alzheimer's must find things to hoard. This is what often leads to the ransacking and possible removal of other people's possessions. This tendency causes great problems in care facilities where some have dementia and others do not. People with dementias often have no sense of possession. They may claim other people's possessions as their own and guard them fiercely, while showing no wish to safeguard what really is theirs. It is a problem but, as with so many other Alzheimer problems, understandable. They have forgotten what is theirs. They may feel other people's things look like theirs, or they may just want to have them and therefore feel they own them.

There is absolutely no point in scolding someone with Alzheimer's for taking things or hoarding or hiding them. It is a memory problem, not a moral problem. It is cruel and meaningless to berate the person for behavior that cannot be helped. If the hoarded objects are important, like a pair of glasses, then have a pair made that only the caregiver has access to. If possible, encourage the person with Alzheimer's to keep things in certain places where you can find them, but do not expect to train the person to do this reliably. People with Alzheimer's cannot reliably learn anything based upon memory alone.

Hygiene

Hygiene becomes a problem for a number of people with Alzheimer's, although it is usually troubling to the caregiver rather than to the sick person, who is no longer aware of the slipping of those formerly well-established habits of cleanliness. Given that we have many judgments attached to our ideas of cleanliness and hygiene, it is important to remember that the sloppiness or downright self-neglect that sometimes develops is only a disease process. The desire to be clean according to the standards of society is not built-in. It is a product of childhood training. Therefore, when disease changes our perceptions and abilities to cope, we forget that training as we forget other things.

Treat the maintenance of cleanliness and hygiene as simply another task with which the person needs help. Do not nag or scold because memory loss has removed that person's former standards. Just deal with it. It is especially important not to scold when incontinence or bowel control is the issue. See the section below on incontinence for a fuller explanation. Cleanliness is likely to be an issue when a person forgets the old routines of showering and washing, cannot or will not change clothes, and is less able to successfully complete toilet habits. All of these may occur as issues as the disease progresses.

At first, verbal reminders might be enough to keep the habit of bathing in place. These should be as non accusatory as possible and couched in the form of gentle bribes.

"Maybe you'd like to have your shower/bath/wash while I make you some coffee."

This works indefinitely for some people, although it may become increasingly necessary to verbally cue every part of the process, one step at a time.

"You could take your clothes off now. That's good. Now maybe you feel like getting into the shower. The water's nice and warm," and so on.

If you use verbal cueing, always remember that the person may not be able to associate words with objects and that you may need to indicate the object you are talking about. Some people show an actual resistance to bathing and washing, rather than simply forgetting to do it. If this is so, you may have to rethink some of your priorities around this issue. Try to understand the resistance. The whole business of bathing and washing may seem overwhelmingly complex to the person with Alzheimer's.

Some people definitely develop a fear of the shower and it is not hard to see why. Maybe people have forgotten that, when they stand under a shower, at some point water will rush out on their heads. There they are, standing peacefully minding their own business when—whoosh!— out comes a violent stream of water. The event is shocking and possibly even unpleasantly stimulating. It is also possible that the beating of water on the head causes brain wave disturbance which activates the fear center.

If someone is afraid of the shower, try running a warm bath instead. Try adding soap bubbles to make it more appealing. This works well for a lot of people. Or try getting them to sit in the shower on a shower stool, and use a hand held shower on them.

Use the shower head in gentle upward movements, avoiding water on the face, talking reassuringly all the time. If this fails, you might try soaking a towel in hot water and wrapping it around the person's body. This feels good and might lead to more feelings of trust developing that would allow you to continue the washing process.

If you are going to wash the person's hair, avoid running water straight onto the head. Instead, place your hand on the person's hair and let the water run on your hand first. This avoids any shock or unpleasant physical feelings about the process.

Whatever methods you try, some people may remain resistant. They may passively resist or they may strike out. It is really not worth your while to create a battle over this any more than you have to. Cut back your requirements for their bathing. Remember anyway that most older people grew up in times when a bath once a week was considered respectable, with a wash and wipe sufficing for everyday cleansing. A good bath or shower once a week really is sufficient for cleanliness, provided you can get some daily cooperation on washing. At a very basic level, as long as people wash under their arms, in the crotch, around the anus, and across the face, they have covered all the potentially smelly areas.

Various people report success with a number of approaches. For example, you could get a big container of baby wipes and persuade your charge to use them for self-cleansing after going to the toilet.

Instead of making bathing or showering a main issue, you could slip it in elsewhere—as a prelude to eating, for example, or before a visit by a beloved friend or relative. You might also consider getting an aide in to help with this task. Some people resist family members helping with bathing because, they feel it is inappropriate, but willingly allow a stranger to help, especially if they think that person is a nurse or medical helper.

One man reports having difficulty with his mother. She felt it was embarrassing for her son to help her with her bathing and she refused to take off her clothes in front of him. Then he said, "It's all right, Mother, I'm a doctor!"

He wasn't, but the trick worked. Mother answered, "Oh, that's all right then," and let him help her off with her clothes. If all else fails, you could try a respite center that includes showers and bathing as part of its routine. Again, strangers might get more cooperation than you do. In the same way, people who hate to have their hair washed might allow it in the context of a hair salon.

One of the major factors in personal cleanliness is cleaning up after going to the toilet. Many people with Alzheimer's eventually forget to do this. Be sure to have the toilet paper where it is visible and easily accessible. Even so, you may still have to give reminders and perhaps hand out toilet paper. You may even have to be prepared to wipe them yourself if need be. If so, put on a vinyl glove, take a good handful of paper and wipe backward, never from the anus forward, since this can introduce infections.

While you may feel this to be humiliating for people with Alzheimer's, the chances are that they will not feel this for themselves. Someone who has gone along far enough to forget to wipe themselves clean has probably also lost the inhibition that made it shameful. In fact, it is no more shameful than needing help with dressing or shopping. It is we who feel it shameful because of the often peculiar attitudes our society has toward elimination and defecation.

If someone is careless with toilet procedure, there will also be a problem of odor and unclean clothing. It is this that people most notice as a process of decline. Try to get clean clothes on your charge every time it is necessary. Carry spare clean underwear with you for a change of clothing away from home.

If the person wants to sleep in soiled clothing, it becomes harder to maintain cleanliness. You will have to be cunning and wait for your opportunity to snatch it away. Some people can only get hold of dirty clothing on the rare occasions they can get their charges into the shower. Others tell the person it is time to get changed for a special occasion or for a visit to the doctor, whether this is true or not. Yet another caregiver managed to get cooperation by saying she had a new item of clothing for the person to wear. A further suggestion: accidentally-on-purpose spill cold water on the offending clothing and it may be easy to get the person to change, although you might have to cope with a catastrophic reaction.

There is no surefire method. Experiment to see what works. If one helper has particular success getting bathing cooperation from your charge, use that person's assistance as often as possible.

Incontinence

This problem is at the great divide of home care. In fact, incontinence is the most-quoted cause of placement in a nursing facility. Therefore, it is worth looking at this problem in depth. First, let us be clear about incontinence. The term is used in general to mean loss of bowel or bladder control, but it is often used incorrectly. Someone who has forgotten to go to the bathroom because of memory loss is not, strictly speaking, incontinent. If a person does not know where the bathroom is anymore or cannot recognize the correct container for toilet purposes and therefore urinates in a waste basket, that is not incontinence.

If a person has become so impaired that he or she cannot recognize the symptoms of needing to urinate or defecate, that is not incontinence. It is dementia. You may think the distinction does not matter, since the results may be the same. However, the important difference is that someone who is impaired by Alzheimer's does not necessarily become incontinent. Even in nursing homes, as much as 90 percent of residents with Alzheimer's need not be incontinent during the daytime, as long as staff regularly take them to the bathroom. The fact that percentages of incontinence are often much higher than 10 percent reflects upon the standard of nursing care.

Home caregivers need to know the heartening news that as many as 90 percent of those with Alzheimer's can remain continent with helpful reminders. A two-hour schedule is adequate for most people, if there are no actual bowel or bladder problems present. Additionally, always ensure that a bathroom visit is made before leaving home and after getting back. It is not necessary to ask if the person wants to go to the bathroom, especially since this may often evoke the answer, "No, I don't need to."

Instead, you will find it more useful to suggest it in a positive way: "Okay, let's just make a bathroom call before we go out!"

If the person denies needing to, just say, "Oh well, why don't you try anyway? We might be out a while."

This works with most people most of the time. However, accidents can always occur. This is where all your tact as a caregiver is needed. Whatever the cause of the incontinence, never berate, scold, or humiliate the person who suffers it. Adults never want to soil themselves. Someone who cannot control elimination functions adequately is not being naughty or willful. It is

172

part of the disease process. Should you make it a major issue, you will create the very stress that leads to loss of control. It is important to remember that our society itself has some odd attitudes about bodily elimination—hence all the strange ritualistic obsessions about toilet training young children. The fact is that children all over the world eventually learn to control their elimination.

However, in our society, incontinence has the triple connotation of being out of control, dirty, and childish. Therefore, we have many warring attitudes within us when it comes to seeing an older person who can no longer exercise these controls. This is why the incontinence factor is major for so many people. One useful thing you could do is to think about it before it ever becomes an issue. Look at ways of coping with it and talk to others who have chosen to deal with it.

Many forms of incontinence clothing are available. You might want to consider what might be most useful. Look at the different kinds of incontinence clothing and adult diapers. If you are not sure which would be suitable, ask your local public nurse to help you decide. Remember that if you are matter-of-fact about it, so will be others. In fact, one man said, "I thought if my wife ever became incontinent, that would be the end of me looking after her. I was sure I couldn't cope with that. When it happened, though, it didn't seem like such a big deal, after all. They have all this special clothing now and it just wasn't the trauma I thought it would be."

He kept his wife at home for a year after she became incontinent. If you are dealing with this problem, remember to keep to the regular schedule of bathroom visits every /two /hours. You also need to get to know the elimination pattern you are coping with, since many people are regular enough that you can work with their pattern. If someone usually has a bowel movement after breakfast or in the afternoon, you can work with that schedule.

At night, you might reduce liquids to a minimum to try to limit nighttime bed wetting. To reduce your own work, think ahead and waterproof the environment in advance. For example, you can put plastic under the covers on the sofa or easy chair in case of accidents. Also, make the bed with plastic under the bed sheet and, if necessary, fold a thick towel across the area where the person's lower body will be positioned. You do not need to buy expensive special equipment. Use garden-strength plastic garbage bags beneath the bottom sheet and a thick bath towel on the sheet. You might think about using diapers just at night in case of accidents.

You will probably eventually have to take on the duty of bathroom reminders, but you may never have to deal with actual incontinence. If it does happen as part of the disease process, it will probably come about gradually. If someone suddenly becomes incontinent, it is more likely a sign of physical or emotional disturbance. Perhaps the person has developed a bladder infection and cannot tell you. Perhaps the problem is due to a change in medication or to sudden stress. Remember that even someone with Alzheimer's can also get other illnesses or medical conditions that cause incontinence.

Get good medical advice and insist on testing for infections or other medical conditions. Ask if prescribed medications can cause incontinence, and double-check elsewhere if your doctor does not seem involved enough. Just because a person has Alzheimer's does not mean that normal medical procedures should be omitted or that the person is entitled to less medical care.

Lastly, do not worry about incontinence before it happens. It may never happen or just be a rare accident, such as when and if a urinary tract infection has developed. Today, with incontinence clothing and a good washing machine, it does not necessarily mean the end of home care if you do not want it to.

On the other hand, neither should you force yourself to deal with it if you feel you cannot. It is a very individual decision and you must respect your own limits.

Paranoia

This is often cited as being one of the problem symptoms of Alzheimer's disease, hence its appearance in this list. However, what might look like paranoia is usually a rational response to living inside the fractured mental abilities brought about by the disease. In other words, it is usually not paranoia but a reasonable fear response, given the limitations of the disease.

"Those people next door came in and stole everything from the kitchen," Suzie tells her son. Anxiously he goes to the kitchen, looks in all the cupboards, and finds everything in the same disarray as usual. Nothing missing.

"Does this mean she's crazy?" he asks his support group. The answer is no. Persons with Alzheimer's fairly commonly think others are stealing from them. The memory problems of the disease mean that people cannot recall what they did with their own possessions and that things seem to have disappeared.

Often, they misinterpret the world around them. Things are misheard or even mistranslated within the mind. As they become fearful and insecure, their sense of safety is eroded. It is personal memory that makes us feel safe. Because of our memory, we know our routine, we know who our friends are, we have a general plan and schedule that directs our lives. The person with Alzheimer's has none of these supports, and it is out of this lack that the often-mentioned paranoia arises. We need to be extremely sensitive to these issues within the lives of those with Alzheimer's. With that sensitivity, we can help create a new sense of security.

That said, it is also possible to have both Alzheimer's and a specific mental illness. The two do not exclude each other, but mental illness is paranoia of another color and a psychiatric consultation is essential. Do not apply the jargon of psychiatry to dementia and do not let non-psychiatrists diagnose your person's alleged mental illness. Always go to the expert.

Privacy

This is a two-edged problem, since both the person with Alzheimer's and the caregiver need privacy. Try to allow the person you are looking after as much privacy as is consistent with comfort. Some people become frightened if left alone even for a few minutes. Be sensitive to any hints that privacy would be enjoyed. If someone sits entirely absorbed in inner thoughts, gazing out of the window at nothing in particular or wandering off into a bedroom, these may be indicators that privacy is wanted. Tiptoe away while your charge is watching television. Go to your room, but leave the door open so you can hear if anything is needed. Sit and silently read a book.

One of the most energy-destroying things you can do is to spend every minute of the day doing something for the person with Alzheimer's. It consumes both of you and is not necessary. It is quite another thing for you to get privacy. You might find you are being followed every minute of the day, even to the toilet, by the person who cannot bear to let you out of sight. This is happening because you represent that person's total emotional security. This is likely to be only a passing phase, you will be relieved to know. Meanwhile, you need to cope with it the way mothers cope with similar attachment by young children.

A wise mother would try to work out why her child is insecure and meet the needs for security. You might try the same. Asking questions might not work, since the impaired person might not be able to verbalize feelings or needs, but you can try it. Then you might try getting the following messages across:

- I understand that life is scary right now.
- I won't leave you.
- You're safe.
- I'll take care of your needs.
- I love you.

Put any of these messages into your own words and keep it simple. Also step up the amount of physical affection and reassurance you give. Hold hands, stroke arms, give back rubs, kiss. Show your affection in a way that is acceptable to the person. Also explain. For example, "I'm going to the bathroom now but I'll be back." Or, "I'm going to put the washing in and I'll be gone for a minute," and so on.

Setting limits is necessary if you are to survive burnout. If it is truly impossible to do that after considerable trial and experimentation, then time off is the only answer. No one lasts for long without private time and private space. Certain kinds of privacy may be almost impossible. Often, persons with Alzheimer's like to fiddle around among other people's possessions. This can be very irritating, but it is only because they do not recognize their own possessions any more. They are not doing it to annoy, but are just curious and all too idle. If you have things you really do not want someone else to meddle with, you must put these objects safely away—for example, in a locked closet.

Psychiatry

Psychiatry unfortunately has little to offer the person with Alzheimer's at this point. Alzheimer's disease is not classified as a mental illness but as an organic disease, and it is actually a disease of function. The language of psychiatry is not even helpful on the whole when applied to the world of the person with Alzheimer's. Psychiatrists are rarely called in, other than as dispensers of medications. The use of psycho-therapeutic intervention is virtually unexplored as yet in the world of Alzheimer's, although there is a strong likelihood that it could help with people's emotional distress.

The reason it is not helpful to apply psychiatric terms like paranoia, delusion, and depression to human beings with Alzheimer's is that to do so discourages caregivers from really listening to the individuals. It encourages dismissal of genuinely felt and soundly based fears and feelings and can suppress relevant response to their unbearable pain. It is helpful to replace certain frequently used psychiatric terms.

For example, replace:
• paranoia with fear
• combative with angry and scared
• depressed with sad, grieving, or lonely
• delusional with misinterpreting
• agitated with fearful
• compulsive (behavior) with under occupied
• perseverating with repeating (questions or phrases)
• wandering with walking
• hallucinating with audio or visual misperception.

The main reason to replace psychiatric vocabulary with non medical terminology is that it puts responsibility for resolving presented problems—such as fear or reactive anger—back where it belongs, on the caregiver. When psychiatric medicines are used to try to control presented problems by suppression instead of by resolution, it is often destructive for the person with Alzheimer's. Almost all such medications carry heavy penalties for the patient with Alzheimer's in the form of toxicity, confusion, agitation, falling, and increased forgetfulness. This may not apply where there is a dual diagnosis—of both Alzheimer's dementia and, for example, psychosis.

There are rare cases where an individual can genuinely benefit from psychiatric medication intervention, but in most cases medication is given for the sake of the caregiver, not because it helps the person with Alzheimer's.

Please note that anti-psychotics are totally inappropriate for regular dementia and in fact, from reports all over the world, are causing the premature death of many elders or permanent irreparable damage.

Repetitive Questions

Repetitive questions are one major reason why people seek help coping with Alzheimer's. There can hardly be anything more likely to drive a caregiver crazy than being asked the same question dozens, scores, or even hundreds of times a day. You may think there is no solution. After all, the essence of this problem is that the person with Alzheimer's does not recall asking the question nor receiving the answer. Nothing can solve that—or can it?

The answer, thank goodness, is that the problem can be solved. Repetitive questions are a common part of the disease process. The form of the question, however, is very significant. The solution lies in paying close attention to the message beneath the question. The essence of this message is usually the same: the need for reassurance, security and love. Everyone has an individual version of the question. It is the specific version that gives the clue to its solution, which lies in answering the need beneath the question.

Here are some examples.

"What time is it?" asks Mr. Da Costa, for the eighth time in an hour.

"Can I go home now?" asks Hannah, sitting in her own home.

"Are my mother and father coming home now?" asks eighty-five-year-old Sophie.

179

When caregivers only answer the literal questions asked, the answer will have to be repeated endlessly. People ask repetitive questions in response to an inner feeling they cannot express, either because they do not recognize it or because they cannot verbalize it. We must look for that feeling, and it is usually not hard to discern. All the feelings that lie beneath repetitive questions really state that this person is lost in the world now. The question usually gives a clue that will reveal the needed answer.

Mr. Da Costa asks what time it is because he is bored and anxious. All the things he used to do are outside his abilities now, and his wife never thinks of asking him to do what little he can. His question is really a statement about how it feels to be stranded in an endless present with nothing to do. People with Alzheimer's have a poor sense of time and they are often under stimulated. Mr. Da Costa's. caregiver could solve this by helping him fill his time. His wife would find relief from hearing that irritating question if she would let him help her— sweep a floor, wash vegetables, wipe a tabletop, do some weeding. He may do none of it very well, but she would get relief from his questions and he would get relief from his consuming boredom.

Hannah asks to go home, even as she sits in her home, because she does not recognize anything around her. Home means familiarity, security, the comfort of routine and habit, of knowing one's place in the world. Because she has Alzheimer's disease, she will never be at home again in the cognitive sense, but she can be helped to feel at home. Her caregiver could deal with this by acknowledging the feeling of loss and strangeness and then offering comfort.

"This is your home. You've lived here about ten years but you forget because you have an illness which makes you forget things," says her caregiver, putting an arm around Hannah. "It must feel very frightening sometimes, but I'm here to help you with anything you need. Maybe you'd like a cup of coffee now, would you? And we could watch your favorite television program. It's on about now."

Sophie asks about her parents because they were her primary relationship. She never married and always lived at home. Although she had a good professional job, she never became emotionally independent. When she feels insecure, she immediately asks about her parents. She too needs love, attention, and something specific to do that can distract her from her feelings of insecurity. Since she always became agitated at night just before dinner, waiting for her parents to come home and eat with her, her caregiver solved this by taking her out to dinner instead.

In looking for the feeling beneath the question, you could ask more questions to elicit what is really bothering the person. Keep trying to find out what the person really wants. if he or she does not cognitively know, make suggestions. To the bored Mr. Da Costa, you might suggest that the two of you take a walk. For the home-seeking Hannah, an activity that makes her feel comfortable might work, such as playing some music she loves. For Sophie, who wants her parents, you might urge her to talk about them or to look at family photographs.

In trying various solutions, you will find what works much of the time. Keep trying and remember that only you will remember the failures, not the person with Alzheimer's. Try not to let repetitive questions get to you. Anger will make compassion impossible and your relationship will deteriorate and may turn into blaming the person who is ill for the very symptoms of the illness. Once you become engaged in the mystery of uncovering their real meaning, you will probably find you have more patience for bearing the questions.

Safety

"I came back and found my wife had put the sheets in the oven and switched it on," says Henry. "I asked her why she did it and she said she was warming them up—which she certainly was!"

Safety is the biggest worry for many caregivers. It has many aspects—keeping someone from wandering away, avoiding fire hazards, watching the use of appliances, and so on. It is very important for every person with Alzheimer's to wear some form of identification. Never assume a person could not walk out of the house and get lost. It does not matter if that has never happened. It only needs to happen once to be a disaster.

Get a Medic-Alert bracelet and have it inscribed with the person's name and phone number and the words "memory impaired." If he or she is ever found wandering and lost, the finder will call the national 800 number on the bracelet or your own phone number. Most people today are familiar with the Medic-Alert system. A bracelet, anklet, or necklace costs $20 and usually takes several weeks to arrive.

Failing that, sew name and phone tags into clothing just as you do for children. You can never assume a person will not become separated from a wallet or handbag, but they are less likely to become separated from their clothing. So, mark the clothing somewhere with identification. Some local police districts are enlightened enough to have a system like that used in Florence, Oregon, a small coastal town with a large elderly population. There they keep a photograph of the person on file and issue a free identification bracelet. If the police in your district do not have such a program, suggest they start one or ask them to keep a picture on file.

Sometimes they will prefer you to keep the photo for use in an emergency. Either way, make sure you do have a clear recent photograph of the person you care for.

Be sure to alert your neighbors too. This is no time for keeping yourself apart from others. Those who have approached their neighbors report getting much help and loving support. Just ask them to let you know if your relative wanders out alone. Often an entire neighborhood becomes a friendly guardian system to help support a family. Safety in the house means childproofing the house for an adult who has had a lifetime of using all the things that suddenly you do not wish him or her to use. Do not waste your energy on trying to retrain the person. It will probably be hopeless. Instead, put your energy into making your house safe.

All stove switches should be off, with the knobs themselves removed if necessary. Gas and electric stoves have one main energy control: use it. Switch the stove off at the main control, and do not ever forget to do it if you are going to leave the person alone in the house. There is a fireproof hood system that will dump chemicals or sand over a stove fire if pots have been left to burn, but this kind of thing does not come cheap. You may find it easier to get the kind of stove that has a lid that can be lowered to cover all burners. It is tedious to do all this but it is safe.

Remove or immobilize all hazards. If the person is no longer able to regulate the shower, for example, turn down your water-heater temperature so no burning can happen. Think of childproofing and you will get the general idea of what to be careful about.

You may need to deal with the driving hazard too. If you have a recalcitrant family member who will not agree to giving up driving, immobilize the car. If you do not know how, ask your friendly garage mechanic to show you the best way to make a car immobile. Most people with Alzheimer's are no longer functional enough to carry out their own car repairs.

The telephone is not usually a hazard, but it can be a source of problems. Its ringing might distress the person, or it might distress you if, in your absence, the telephone is answered strangely. Turn down the bell and put on an answering machine for when you are not handy. If you find your relative gets disturbed or angry when you talk on the telephone, think about getting an extra extension so you can go into another room and talk privately. Or use a cell for all private business. Many families report this problem. It is hard to know whether the telephone is too abstract for the patient to understand, or whether it is the lack of attention that agitates. Avoid the confrontation anyway, whatever that problem really is.

Under safety comes medications. Never trust the person with Alzheimer's to take medication in the right quantities. Measure the dose out instead and then put it away. If there is resistance to taking it, suggest the doctor ordered it or that it is vitamins—whatever works. If you think you see adverse reactions to new medications, report them to your doctor. Persons with Alzheimer's are notoriously sensitive to the effects of medicine and disease, so be confident in what you see. If you are disturbed by it, your doctor should be too. If you cannot get the right responses from your doctor, get a new doctor, but meanwhile call your pharmacist.

The major aspect of house safety is keeping the person under surveillance and natural hazards around the house out of reach. For surveillance, there are a host of door alarms available to warn you if the person leaves the house. Or you may make do simply with a necklace of bells hanging on the door. While the fire department usually does not recommend locking doors from the inside, because of the fire hazard, you may want to limit access to doors out of the house. Use your common sense and be aware of fire hazards. Even a simple slip lock can effectively make it hard for the person with Alzheimer's to figure a way out without being dangerous in case of fire.

Sexual Inappropriateness

This is less common than people think but it is frequently mentioned by caregivers as something they fear happening. First, realize that some things which appear sexual are not. Many people with Alzheimer's fiddle with their clothes. This is often because they have too little to do and therefore get fidgety. Conversely, they may also suffer from over stimulation in the brain itself. It is also possible that the clothes are uncomfortable and that soft warm sweats would be much better than the tight shiny polyesters that many older people wear.

Women may undo their blouses or adjust their underclothes without inhibition, and men may undo their trouser zippers. These are not sexual actions nor intended to be provocative. They are simply the result of idly wandering hands. The best solution is to find something for those hands to do. You could give a known fidgeter a set of beads, for example, like the worry beads that Greeks and Turks carry with them. More rarely, men and sometimes women with Alzheimer's may expose themselves. This, too, is inadvertent. Their action is socially inappropriate but not actually sexual. Suggest they stop doing it. Often such action is a sign that they wish to go to the bathroom but cannot communicate the need. In some cases, it may even be a sign that there is some genital or urinary discomfort due to infection. If this kind of activity starts suddenly, it needs to be checked out by the doctor.

Occasionally a man with Alzheimer's (less often a woman) will actually make what is clearly a sexual advance, by placing a hand on someone's breast or thigh, for example. In these cases, the correct response is simply to remove the offending hand and explain calmly that this is not acceptable. The usual social inhibitions against such behavior are being eroded by brain disease. It is not the outrage it would be from a fully cognitive person. It is just

185

the expression of the fact that sexuality still lives as a vital force in that person.

In one care home, a ninety-two-year-old woman was renowned for squeezing the thigh of the man who came to do everyone's hair. Since the man was amused rather than outraged, he never said anything to her about it.

Sexuality

People do not necessarily lose their sexuality or their capacity to express it until the later stages of Alzheimer's. A married couple may still have a full sexual life together, and an unmarried person can continue affairs with great success. Some find this shocking. They think that, for example, a man should not want to make love to his impaired wife. Sometimes adult children feel they should prevent an impaired parent from forming a sexual relationship with another adult. This comes out of our general feeling in this society that people who are disabled are not, or should not be, or should not even want to be, sexual beings—-even more so if they are old and disabled.

It is nonsense to think or suggest that people who have disabilities or illnesses should be forbidden to have a sexual life. They may have very satisfactory sexual relationships. How a married couple work out their sexuality isn't anyone's business but their own. The sexual drive often remains as whole as it formerly was; just as the sense of humor remains whole, spirituality and the ability to enjoy a number of life's pleasures remain with the person with Alzheimer's. There can indeed be fun after Alzheimer's, and some of it may well be sexual. The duty of the children of a parent with Alzheimer's extends only as far as ensuring that the parent is not being abused or ill used. If a parent can form and maintain a relationship to the satisfaction of the two people most involved, the children should be very happy about it, rather than using the occasion for censorship.

A far more frequent problem that arises in families comes when the impaired spouse is placed in full-time care and the other spouse starts to want to establish a relationship with an outside partner. This is a complex matter that basically should be left to the individual concerned. Unfortunately, often the adult children expect the unimpaired spouse to sit alone night after night in an empty house that is no longer a home. Yet those same adult children give little of their own time to the healthy parent. That is a heavy additional burden of loneliness for an already suffering human being to carry.

Sleep

Sleep problems in Alzheimer's are actually waking problems, the most frequent being the nighttime wakefulness that affects some people. Often the person with Alzheimer's loses all sense of time. Even though he or she can still read the time on a clock, it does not mean anything cognitively any more. So, when the person wakes up, he or she gets up and dresses and is ready to go out, in spite of the fact that it may be pitch-dark and only three in the morning. This usually happens when considerable impairment has already affected the person.

It is no use to ask, "Why did you get up?" Pointing out that it is night and therefore time to sleep probably will not work either. The person may get up in the night on impulse through lack of tiredness, because it just feels like time to get up, to go to the bathroom, to explore, to get something to eat or drink—for all kinds of reasons.

It scarcely matters what the reason is. What matters is what you are going to do about it. There is no reason why someone cannot wander about the house at night as long as there is no danger involved. The ideal sleepless situation is the night-waker who is content to patter around the bedroom without trying to leave. The worst is the person who wakes you at three in the morning

187

demanding to be taken shopping. The ideal response to that would be to do exactly that, but many of us are not at our best and most cooperative at 3am. In those cases, negotiate the person back to bed if you can. Perhaps a gentle back rub will help, or glass of hot milk and a cookie, or soothing music. Sometimes people awake to go to the bathroom and either cannot find it or forget what they wanted to do and start in on other activities.

The real problem with sleeplessness is not how it affects the person with Alzheimer's—who, after all, can sleep the next day—but how it affects the caregiver. You have to be able to sleep. No one can go long with interrupted nights, especially if there is stressful daytime work to be done. If possible, get substitute caregivers to sleep overnight so that you can sleep. If that is impossible, you may finally have to resort to sleeping medication for your charge, but be aware that it comes at great cost. There are few satisfactory major sleep medications for people with Alzheimer's. They all have unfortunate side effects, some of which can greatly increase the confusion, agitation, and impairment of the disease. Remember, an active day is the best forecaster of a quiet night.

Undressing
Some people go through a stage of taking off their clothes in public, and this can be understandably hard for caregivers to deal with. It is not hard for people with Alzheimer's to deal with since they have no sense that it is not appropriate. We can only guess why they do this. Maybe it feels good to be naked, perhaps their clothes are uncomfortable, possibly they are simply expressing some kind of emotional vulnerability, or they simply need something interesting to do.

It is a hard problem to deal with, since the urge seems to be quite persistent while it is present. Nursing homes often have dealt with it by either tying people up or drugging them into submission, both of which are extremely questionable in terms of medical ethics and are now illegal in all states. Some caregivers solve the problem by adapting. They draw the blinds or curtains in the house and let the person be naked. Others get clothes that are hard for the person to remove—long dresses or robes for women, pants fixed up with suspenders at the back for men. It is certainly worth exploring getting sweatpants and tops anyway, since these are soft and comfortable to wear. You might find an outfit that would be hard for the person to take off. Some clothing made for the disabled could be useful, the kind that is fastened at the back instead of the front.

You could probably adapt some clothes so that they have extra zippers and fastenings, some of which you could secure with a tiny padlock or pin.

Not many people seem to want to take their clothes off outside, because they are distracted by their surroundings. If they are inclined to disrobe, keep them moving, keep them eating, keep them occupied doing something until you can get them safely home where they are free to undress in the safety of their own private environment. If this seems shocking, remember that nudity really is only a social embarrassment (and possibly a minor legal offense). If you have visitors who might be shocked, try confining the person with Alzheimer's to some other room while the visitors are there. Or enlist the help of your visitors by explaining the situation to them, since they are often likely to be compassionate and understanding.

Do not under-estimate the basic discomfort of many of the kinds of clothes elders wear. Old ladies typically have worn polyester clothing for decades but these are not necessarily that comfortable for a more sedentary lifestyle. Neither are dresses and skirts. It may be time to consider trying to persuaded an elderly woman into comfortable soft pants instead – and good luck with that.

Wandering

"Reward: $10,000 for any information on Walter Harris, aged eighty-two, who wandered away from his home on Friday, July 13. If you see this man, call his son at. . ."

This is the nightmare of every caregiver and the most common problem mentioned by caregivers. That does not mean it is the most common occurrence in Alzheimer's, since by no means does everyone become a wanderer.

It just means that, when a caregiver does have to deal with wandering, it is seen as a major problem. It is easy to see why. A person who has Alzheimer's may be unable to find his or her way home and could be missing for days. Others may lack judgment about walking across highways and put themselves in grave physical danger. Either way, when someone with Alzheimer's disappears, whether briefly or for hours or days, it is a tremendous worry for the caregiver.

There are several approaches to this problem, but before we look at them, let us remind ourselves of a truth all too often forgotten – you or I can leave our house anytime we want to and no one will classify us as wanderers. The person with Alzheimer's once had that same freedom to go for a walk anytime, anywhere. That entirely natural freedom is one of the many losses resulting from having the disease.

Our problem as caregivers is that we have a custodial role to keep our charges safe. People who go into nursing facilities are often treated as troublemakers when they want to get out of the door, but they are merely trying to exercise a normal human freedom that their illness has now robbed them of. Any sensible person would want to leave a nursing home. It is a warm, cozy prison where you go for no crime except that of getting old or sick and there is no time off, no matter how good you are. So, let us remember that just as weeds are only plants growing where we do not want them, so wandering is only walking that we do not want to occur.

The first important thing to do is to make sure that if a person with Alzheimer's does wander away, there is some identifying item on the person. This cannot just be in a wallet or a pocket, since that is not secure or even safe from the interference of the person with dementia. It could be a medical style ID bracelet or a dog tag. If your person interferes with these, consider an ankle tag. These days, we can also slip a personal GPS tag on a person. At the back of the pants, on a sock or shoes – you can experiment until you find a secure placing for this. Such systems are around the hundred dollar mark and well worth it.

Assuming that identification has been secured, then it is time to deal with the problem of wandering. Most of us get restless when confined to our homes, and people with Alzheimer's are no exception to this. They need to get out and about for exercise and stimulation. It is also clearly a way in which many people with dementia self-medicate their anxiety and fear and it is a very valuable tool for helping them adjust to an emotionally very difficult health condition. It is essential that they walk two or three times a day, as long as they can physically manage this. Ideally you or another caregiver would walk with them or perhaps track along behind them.

In the early stages, you may be able to allow your charge considerable freedom to roam if you know that he or she can find the way home or can be easily electronically tracked. One family managed to convince their mother never to go beyond a certain point at the end of their block. Yet another family was able to arrange for their mother to walk to and fro between two family homes situated near each other. All of these were satisfactory solutions and met the person's need for exercise and even gave some welcome freedom. It is always possible to trail behind someone who decides to go for a walk and just catch up when you sense that it is time to intervene.

If you need to know when your charge leaves home, use alarms or bells on the front door or simple keep it locked. One man reports great success with painting grille like stripes in front of the door. His wife, with the distorted perception common to Alzheimer's, refuses to step on them because she suspects that they are bars she might fall through. Another family painted a big red STOP sign on the inside of their front door to remind their mother not to leave the house.

Most people are ready for a walk when they want to leave the house. That is why they are trying to leave. Take them for walks and give them that sense of freedom. Sometimes, however, people want to go for walks at inconvenient times, like 2 A.M. Usually this is because their sense of time has completely gone and they are no longer cognitively aware that nighttime is not the appropriate time for going out. If you know they cannot get out of the house – because you have safely unopenable locks in place -- you can simply let your person wander. It does not actually matter if they are wakeful or restless. If you are prepared to do it, you can even take them out shopping in the middle of the night if you have an all-night store near you.

Most people with Alzheimer's who walk a lot do so to calm themselves. It is a practical way to deal with the stress and tension that this disease creates within. Every person who can walk should do so, taking three or four good walks a day. It is good for physical and emotional health and it will be good for you, the caregiver, too. Adapt the walks to the taste of the person. You might walk through museums, through shopping malls, several times around the block, along the beach, or beside a nursery school — whatever works for you both.

Many of your daily problems reduce when you keep your family member busy and occupied. Therefore, make activity plans that help to pass the time pleasantly. If you cannot do this, go to the day-activity program in your area or arrange for someone to take over some activities with your family member. You will find it really helps.

CHAPTER NINE

LOVE WORKS

You may not be expecting to find a chapter on love in a care- giving book, but it is here because love is the greatest resource in living with Alzheimer's disease. Apart from all its other difficulties, Alzheimer's usually involves a great crisis of love, both on the part of the person who has the disease and on the part of all those who live with or are involved with it.

The person who has Alzheimer's disease has an undisguised yearning for love and is often as open as a child to the longings of the heart. In this sense, we could say that Alzheimer's disease turns into a journey from the mind to the heart. Typically, people with Alzheimer's express their longings for deep emotional security and unconditional love all the time. Often, we may not choose to hear what they say. Either at home or in care , it is typical for these words to be dismissed as the babbling of dementia, but if we stop and listen, we can hear the longings clearly expressed.

"I want to go home."

"I want to see my mother."

"I'm lonely."

"No one ever comes to see me."

These are not just nonsense or meaninglessly repeated complaints. They are the deepest longings of the human being—to be cared for and accepted, to be cherished and protected, to be loved. We are face to face with the profound human hunger for unconditional love. That can make many of us feel uncomfortable or inadequate, especially if we face at the same time our inability to really give love in such a manner.

There are many relationships of conditional love. In fact, they are much more common than those of unconditional love. For example, married love may well depend upon decades-long exchanges between husband and wife. These exchanges are often connected with accepting roles, carrying through perceived duties, finding a basis for gratifications. When one partner can no longer carry through these arrangements, a crisis of love arises. The partner becomes impatient, angry, feels trapped because a certain sense of orderliness has been disrupted and a lifestyle thrown into chaos.

An adult child finds the same problems emerging when a parent has Alzheimer's. The perceived task of a parent is to nurture, to be protective and concerned, to give love to the child, to be unchanging and faithful in the parental role. If that parent should begin instead to ask for nurturing, for protection, for a parental type of love from the child, a crisis of love can come about. What do we do about it? Often, what family members do is to search for care to be given, instead of dealing with the crisis of love. Either the family member becomes totally involved in personally providing care, or becomes caught up in trying to obtain care in other ways.

Maybe searching for the right nursing home, the perfect caregiver, even moving to another part of the country because the right kind of care might exist there. Much of this desperate searching is really connected with the fact that a crisis of love has arisen that is not being dealt with. Sometimes it is because a crisis of love has finally been revealed—for example, if a child had still secretly been hoping that a parent would turn into the earned-for mother or father, Alzheimer's means the end of such dreams. The person with Alzheimer's disease gives us perfect opportunities to practice unconditional love and compassion.

If we can really understand the childlike terrors that awaken an old woman in the night, instead of being impatient with being awakened ourselves, we feel

196

compassion. If we really comprehend the confusion of not knowing what day it is, not knowing a face around us, not recognizing anyone we love, we feel tenderness and protectiveness. When this other human being appears to us unprotected and vulnerable, plainly needing our help, we are touched by that need.

Or so we might hope. The reason we so often fail as caregivers to have this understanding and to feel this compassion is certainly not that we are bad people—far from it. If we are trying to be caregivers, it is out of our innate goodness. We fail most often because we do not allow the time that love needs. We fill up our day with a thousand different caregiving duties and demands, many of which are frankly not even important, because so often we are avoiding our own inner feelings of pain.

We have no sense of proportion about what matters because we forget the importance of love. If the person you care for died tonight, what would you rather be able to say tomorrow: "Well, at least his clothes got washed so I can bury him in clean ones," or "Thank goodness we sat and held hands together while the sun went down"? The answer probably is obvious when we read the words, but we often tend to lose this perspective.

Alzheimer's gives us unique opportunities to deal with the issues of love—unconditional, compassionate love, unattached to any expectations, duties, or rewards other than the bliss of being in that wonderful flow for a while. None of the conditional love pictures fit.

The person with Alzheimer's cannot be your mother if she is living in the memory of being sixteen and thinks you are her brother. The woman who is your wife cannot do the washing, cleaning, cooking, and shopping duties with any accuracy with Alzheimer's disease. How, then, will you find it in yourself to love this person?

One way is to let go of our expectation of the roles that this person used to fill and simply accept the present

197

moment. This is very hard for most of us to do. Without even thinking about it, we are totally attached to the roles we expect people to play. We find it hard to let go of our expectations. Much of our love for someone is attached specifically to that person's particular role. In Alzheimer's, people forget their roles, and those around them find it hard to forgive or accept. Instead, they stay attached to some other time, some other situation, never living in the now.

Yet there is no other reliable moment in Alzheimer's. The past may be forgotten, the future has no reality, but there is here and now. Being loving with someone in the here and now, with no past or future pictures, no conditional behavior pictures, is both very hard and extremely easy. It is hard because we seldom give up our mind-created pictures of what we want from a person or what we expect or how we judge. It is hard because our minds are usually running here, there, and anywhere but in this place called the now. At the same time, it is easy because we only have to sit there and hold hands lovingly and think and be love. It is so little to give, and doing it is like reaching across a great ocean.

A family member may be loving and accepting with a child and yet be unable to accept the same behavior in an adult.

"Yes, I can accept this in my four-year-old, but not in my father-in-law," says Linda. Yet there is no difference between child and father-in-law in their need for love. The difference is in Linda. Love is both the central crisis of Alzheimer's and the path for spiritual development in the caregiver. This seems particularly fitting because Alzheimer's disease obviously involves a sense of psycho-spiritual crisis. If the crisis did not exist before—and almost invariably it did—it certainly comes about within the illness. The phrase psycho-spiritual crisis means that a person is living without inner resources, without a real inward sense of being whole, often exhausted by a lifetime in which few needs have been met. Often the crisis involves early deprivation and loss never resolved.

It often comes about in a human being who has never had the chance to become himself or herself, who has been buried in roles and the expectations of others. In a person whose system is already being overwhelmed, as in Alzheimer's disease, a complete dissolution comes about. We see this again and again in the development of Alzheimer's. Nearly every major manifestation of the disease follows some trauma—accident, loss, another illness, displacement, a fall, mugging, burglary, a car crash, an operation involving general anesthesia. Major manifestation means the marked loss of capacity to function in everyday life. Many people get along— falteringly, but they do get along—until some trauma intervenes. Then, family members report, severe Alzheimer's symptoms appear and they are no longer able to get along.

A survey of an Alzheimer care unit in the San Francisco Bay area revealed that of the 54 patients in the unit, a startlingly high number had been teachers, nurses, social workers, and caregivers. All their lives, these residents had been people whose time had been given to the nurturing of others. A significant number had also undergone lives of considerable crisis and deprivation, especially when they were children. Some were starved and beaten as children, raped, molested, put in concentration camps, orphaned, and abandoned. Others had been abused continually as adults, had undergone treatment with psychiatric medications, or had been victims of crimes of violence. The degree of drama in those lives had been markedly high.

Aside from all the genetic and environmental factors that may be involved in this disease, it seems connected also with inner crisis. Just as we now have medically accepted the concept that there is a personality type prone to heart attack and stroke—the hypertensive "Type A" person—and stress-related personality traits linked to cancer, perhaps there is a nurture-hungry yearning group of people who are at increased risk of developing Alzheimer's. Perhaps this is the extra predisposing factor that causes some people to fall victim to Alzheimer's.

Many of us love in a fairly small-scale way—that is to say, we probably love for exchange, for control, for gratification, out of duty, or out of some inner emptiness that we seek to fill. Loving someone with Alzheimer's unconditionally can introduce us to a much larger way of loving and can put us in touch with an entirely different set of values.

We cannot experience that as long we are too frightened to really look at this illness. We cannot do it while we are too angry to be able to sit down and really be with the person. We cannot do it when we are so consumed by what lies within us that we cannot sit still. If we can practice letting go, being here in the present moment, reaching out with compassion, and just letting flow happen, everything gets easier.

This kind of loving is not sentimental, airy-fairy, pie-in-the-heavenly-sky stuff. It is the most practical and rewarding way to get through an Alzheimer day. Using love—real, unconditional love—works. It works better than drugs, shouting at someone, or scolding. It is an efficient way of managing difficult behaviors.

Your doctor might not think of telling you to try unconditional love as a way of dealing with Alzheimer crisis, but as a caregiver, you will find it works. Instead of fighting to control the person, you let go and—surprise!—the battle is over. You can get someone with Alzheimer's to do what you want as soon as you stop wanting it. It is the tension of the two of you wanting that keeps the resistance up and, for example, stops your husband from being able to put his sweater on properly. Your emotional tension causes confusion and dysfunction in your relative.

If you cannot let go of your mother being your mother, she will continue to call you "Mother" because she feels the loneliness of you withholding love. Whatever you think you are hiding inside you will be reflected back by the person with Alzheimer's. That is what makes Alzheimer's so uncomfortable for others to be with. Women who were always meek and obedient to their husbands show their anger. Men who were strong, silent, take- charge types weep. Those with Alzheimer's often show us part of ourselves we prefer not to deal with.

If you can relax and lovingly be with someone in the here and now, you will experience an expansion, a warmth, an exchange of deep love that will really feed you. Unconditional love is not a measure, it is a flow. You cannot give it or get it, you can only be a part of it. When you love a person with Alzheimer's in this way, clarity and awareness often come to that person.

Again, as hard to believe as this may be, countless numbers of caregivers can attest to this. When you can really love your mother exactly as she is, she can reemerge and be who she used to be for a while. It happens all the time. It is not really hard to understand. We know in general that even normal people become nervous, agitated, or depressed around other nervous, agitated, or depressed people. We human beings do not live as islands, as poet John Donne once reminded us. We are in constant communication about how we feel, whether we wish to be or not.

If you and your spouse are unhappy, your children will manifest unhappiness too, no matter how careful you are to be kind to them. The person with Alzheimer's is notprotected by all the barriers that most of us erect against the things we do not wish to know or see, but is very sensitive to the feelings of others. If you are not ready to read or hear this, it is okay to turn the page, but what is here will haunt you anyway. If you do not have it in you yet, you will always feel pinched and small hearted and echo emptily within. If you can just sit and try some of this, you will experience great changes.

How do you try unconditional love? Sit still and do nothing except be. Look for the yearning for love however it is expressed by that person you know so well. Does the stubborn set of the shoulders tell you this person is frightened to let the need show? Are the eyes questioning and fearful? Is the body rigidly fixed into no-one-can-ever-hurt-me toughness? Is the face an iron mask that hides all feelings? If so, what is the deepest feeling you imagine hiding behind the mask?

Where is the child inside who never had enough love, enough care, sometimes even enough food or safety? Can you see that child? Can you feel compassion for that child at all? Did this person ever tell you about the toughness, the sadness, the disappointments of early life? Can you now forgive everything you never had from this person? If you can, that will heal your own hurts because it allows you to experience unconditional love. Any time you do, it flows back in time to all your wounds and heals them.

If you feel sad when you try this, that would be appropriate. People suffer greatly in this world and our compassion makes us feel sad for them. As we feel sad for them, so we inevitably reflect back to any sadness we have for our own suffering in this life. Most of the suffering you read and hear about in connection with Alzheimer's is not the suffering of the person with the disease. It is the suffering of the family.

"Bill would have hated to be somewhere like this," says his wife, standing in the nursing home where Bill has been put into care. "His sister had Alzheimer's and he always said he'd hate to end up like her."

Actually, at that very moment, Bill was happily walking around trying to organize a group to take part in a musical activity. He was cheerful and upbeat, as he was every day without fail. The Bill who hated the idea of Alzheimer's had been forgotten; this Bill was content and busy with self-appointed fantasy activities that pleased him immensely. His wife suffered every time she came to see him because she was still relating to that gone-away Bill. For her, he was endlessly suffering even though he was demonstrably happy.

Although it sounds harsh to say so, Bill's wife was deluded in her thinking at this point. She was trapped in the past. In that, she was typical of many Alzheimer families.

Until we deal with these issues honestly, we will never create an emotional ability to deal with Alzheimer's. The nationwide inability to do so is killing families, killing caregivers, killing people in the heart, if not also in the body. If we do not deal with our issues of love and grief around the failures of love, we cannot live with Alzheimer's disease. We are fortunate as caregivers because we get the rare opportunity to practice love every day. We step into that flow as soon as we do the smallest act of love. We can do it any time. Just tuck an arm around your relative or hold a hand, or gently and steadily rub a shoulder and really think your love into that person as you do it.

Try consciously letting go of your disappointment and anger and need, even for a moment or two. Breathe it out and let it go instead of holding it tight and pinched inside you. If there are things you want to say, say them.

"I hate it that you have this illness."

"I can't stand it that we can't live the way we used to."

"It's not fair that we can't have our golden years the way we planned."

"I miss you being my mother now that I have to look after you so much."

"You were a lousy father to me but I love you anyway."

Or even, "It's really hard for me to love you when you were such a lousy father."

Say whatever you want to, knowing that it will be completely forgotten by tomorrow and will not be held against you. If you find it hard to speak so honestly, imagine that this person will be dead tomorrow—which is always possible—and ask yourself, "What would I have wished to have said?"

Do not allow yourself to be overtaken by your anger. Speak with compassion and forgiveness. Practice them all the time. Practice stillness. Practice love.

Love works.

CHAPTER TEN

WHAT SHALL WE DO NEXT?
AN ACTIVITY GUIDE

Boredom is one of the worst problems that affects people with Alzheimer's in daily life. It underlies many of the behavioral problems that trouble caregivers. Since those with Alzheimer's often have plenty of energy but lack the capacity to continue their former activities, they face a constant struggle to find enough ways to pass the time. As they depend so much upon caregivers, this becomes the caregiver's battle too. Old habits may not survive, so new ones have to be created. Finding what works is a matter of trial and error.

As a caregiver, you already have many demands upon your time. To also be the source of full-time entertainment can be too much. In this section you will find suggestions for a variety of activities to occupy those with Alzheimer's. It is arranged in alphabetical order for easy reference. You do not have to do all this – involve other people. Those people who offer to help? Get them to take your person for a nice drive, an ice cream or play cards badly. Never turn down an offer of help. Show people what to do and largely they love to do it. Try them and see.

Artwork

Art activity is ideal for people who are suffering the verbal and rational thinking impairment typical of Alzheimer's disease. It is also easy to do at home and can take many forms, from buying a coloring book and set of colored pens or pencils, to more elaborate drawing or painting. Some people will reject it as childish but many people like passing the time this way.

If a caregiver can give the time to joining in, the art activity will be even more successful. Clay work is satisfying for many impaired people, as is cutting out shapes or arranging designs. If you are short of ideas, go to a good toy shop and search for ideas there. They will also offer a full selection of non- toxic art supplies available. Many of the art projects that work with young children will also appeal to those with Alzheimer's disease, since—although they certainly do not become like children—they may return to certain primal modes of ability, interest, and pleasure.

Books

Books can be a great source of pleasure even for the person who can no longer read or who seems to have lost interest in reading. Many people with Alzheimer's become apathetic about reading. When actually asked to read something they will do so, but it is almost as if they do not really take in what they read. They may be affected by brain changes that make it hard for them to comprehend as well as complete the task of reading.

It may be that trying to follow a story or plot line is becoming too abstract an idea or is too hard to retain in the failing memory. Even so, people who had the habit of reading may still enjoy the feeling of sitting with a book of their own beside a caregiver who is also reading a book of his or her own. The peaceful normality of such an act often seems very calming.

Even if a person has obviously limited ability to read, it can still be possible to use books extensively. Try getting illustrated books from the library on subjects that have always interested the person—travel pictures for the traveler, animal books for the pet lover, and so on. Looking through such a book together can trigger memories and stories as well as passing time pleasantly in the present.

If adult books become too hard, try material from the juvenile section of the library. Well-illustrated children's books are not usually perceived as being childish by the person with Alzheimer's, and they can provide a lot of enjoyment. Often they encourage the person to read aloud to the caregiver. Poetry can be very successful, even with people who never enjoyed it before. Its rhythm and cadence is pleasing to many with Alzheimer's. Funny verse is accepted as well, since the sense of humor remains unimpaired no matter how severe the stage of the Alzheimer's. If you are not familiar with possible choices of reading matter, ask your librarian, who will undoubtedly be delighted to help.

People have tried using books on tape with varied success. Some people are not able to maintain concentration long enough to follow a story, others love it.

Make use of any storytelling performances in your area. For example, many public libraries have a story hour for children, and impaired people often enjoy this. The material is understandable to them, and usually they greatly enjoy the presence of children. Most librarians are willing for an older impaired person to be present at such readings. Should the older person feel uneasy at being present among children, say that you just wanted a chance to enjoy being with children for a while.

Cooking

This must be a supervised activity, but it can be fun to do. Many people with Alzheimer's can be handy in the kitchen by helping to prepare food. Cutting, chopping, mixing, and stirring are possible activities. Try simple recipes, the type that might be suitable for young children. If you are out of ideas, look at a children's cookbook at your library or local bookstore. Making cookies is often a great success, since the results come out quickly and can be immediately consumed.

Simple meals can be prepared together, such as soup and sandwiches or a salad and cold cuts. Obviously, it is necessary to keep an eye on the use of knives and cutters, and people who are combative may not be able to deal with the limitations and frustrations of work in the kitchen. Use commonsense. And do not push away these possibilities by saying, "I could do this faster by myself." Of course you could.

But then your person would have spent yet another long boring day with nothing to do. You don't have to think up special out-of-hosue activities. You are doing activities all day long. Just make a little space for your person to contribute

Dancing

Many people who used to dance can still do it remarkably well even with severe Alzheimer's. It is one of those abilities that seem to stay whole. Feet apparently do not forget to dance. At home, you can pop on a familiar piece of dance music and take
a person for a whirl around the floor. It is fun and, of course, good exercise.

One son who is a full-time caregiver to his mother takes her dancing on Friday evenings. She loves the time out and is a popular partner because she is good at dancing. Since she, like many people with Alzheimer's, has a good fund of small talk, no one has ever seemed to notice her general state of impairment. The exercise also helps reduce her periods of wakefulness during the night. Good dancers are always in demand. It might be possible for you to ask another dancer to take the person with Alzheimer's to a dance at a senior center.

Day Centers

Day-care and respite programs for people with Alzheimer's are one of the best supports available for caregivers. Many people do not understand their value, both to the person with Alzheimer's as well as to the caregiver.

Many family members simply do not understand what day care is like. Many older people seem to equate taking some- one to day care with abandoning them to the workhouse, while younger people have probably never visited either a senior center or a day-care program in their lives. Both need to educate themselves.

"I feel so guilty when I take Mother to the respite program," Gwen says. "But she's much less depressed now and she's willing to get up in the mornings, that wasn't true before. I just wish I felt better about it."

Of course we cannot tell Gwen this, but her mother has much more fun at the day center than she ever has at home. Day care offers people with Alzheimer's what their family members often cannot or will not offer. It provides an interesting daily program of activities much more varied than what is available at home. And this happens in a nonjudgmental, caring atmosphere where there is no failure.

Family members tend to forget just how much a person with Alzheimer's is reminded every hour of every day that he or she can no longer live a normal life. In a day-care center, it is different. A typical day-care program offers exercise, artwork, cooking, singing, dancing, games, and unconditional love and acceptance from those working there. People can spend time with others dealing with the same problems, in various stages of the illness. They can help each other and share their feelings about things.

Annie and Grace always sit next to each other at the respite program. They can often be seen talking intently together, Annie patting Grace's hand or Grace stroking Annie's hair.

Annie says, "So I told them you can't make a monkey out of me," while Grace is saying, "And those flowers out there are just—well, they're—I don't."

They may not be involved in coherent dialogue, but they are involved in a supportive relationship with each other. Something good happens for them that is not cognitive but does have emotional power.

It is true that at first many persons with Alzheimer's feel trepidation at entering such a program. They may say they do not want to go or refuse to let their caregiver leave, but these adjustment problems tend to vanish very soon in most cases. The period of adjustment is similar to that experienced by a young child entering preschool or kindergarten for the first time.

It is often not long before the program becomes a vital part of life. Even though the person may forget where he or she has been during the day, the family can see an improvement in spirits, in involvement in life, and in general attitude. Caregivers often report that former depression or sleep problems go away when a person becomes part of a regular supportive day-care program. Being busy all day allows the person to get pleasantly tired, thus leading to a full night's sleep.

It also helps to restore lost self-esteem and exposes the person to the kind of tension-free atmosphere that is often no longer possible at home.

Good centers encourage family members to stay around to see that all is well and happily give reports on progress or discuss how to manage any problems that arise. Most centers report that the ones who have difficulty in separating are not the people with Alzheimer's but their caregivers. Overworked caregivers often manifest their stress by being unable to let go of the person they look after. They fantasize that the person cannot manage without them, even for an hour or a day. This is nonsense, and it is unhealthy.

If that describes you, you need a good rest. Do yourself and the person you look after a favor and help them to enter a good day-care program. Both of you will get time off from each other. Finding good adult daycare calls for the same kind of investigation you would undertake to find good day care for your child, and the criteria are similar. Look for a number of the following:

• bright, cheerful interior;
• reasonable amounts of space;
• high ratio of staff to attendees;
• well-trained, sensitive staff who treat people with respect, affection, and understanding;
• a varied program offering different activities for different levels of ability;
• evidence of participants' work on the walls;
• display of photographs and biographies of the participants, so each person is recognized as an individual.

It is essential that the center be equipped to deal with wanderers or those who want to leave the building. It is not unusual for people to want to leave a center, especially if they are new to the program. It is a natural reaction. The center should be equipped with doors that have alarms on them so that no one can wander away unseen, or there should be enough staff so that one person can be free to give time to the wanderer who feels an urgent need to get out, go home, or get away.

Ideally, although this is not always possible, there should be a safe walking area outside the building so that wanderers and those who need to walk a lot can do so. This shows that the staff are willing to let some people withdraw from activities if they wish to, thus respecting their individuality.

Things to check on:
• Will staff take the attendee to the bathroom regularly?
• Is an attendee allowed to sit out activities?
• How does the staff deal with wanderers?
• Do they encourage people to eat for themselves or do they hurry them by feeding them?

Although many centers will cite a set fee that may be outside your budget, ask if they have a sliding scale. Many centers are funded from public foundations and health authorities and are supposed to be available for those with lower incomes.

Allow time for adjustment. If there are definite signs of distress that have not declined within a month, it may be that day care is not for your person. However, that is very rare and usually tends to occur only when the move to day care took place too late for easy adjustment. Most people gain from a day-care program. Their lives become richer and therefore they are happier and better adjusted emotionally.

Even if you are dealing with someone who would never have gone to such a center before Alzheimer's, do not assume it cannot be successful now. Try it first and give it a fair chance, then decide whether to continue. The only person I know of who did not adjust well to the day-care experience had spent many years living independently and was also probably too impaired to become part of a group at the late stage of her disease. Many people recover sociability—or even show it for the first time.

Driving

This refers to caregiver driving, since people with Alzheimer's should not be driving at all. Many caregivers observe that this is one of the most successful ways of amusing people with Alzheimer's. It is safe, enclosed, and entertaining in an undemanding way, interesting and yet soothing at the same time. Head for a green and peaceful area, or drive to an ice cream parlor.

Use driving to deal with mood changes and anger, too, since it seems to be soothing for most people. Keep the speed down, since high speeds make many people nervous and sudden stops are frightening for them. For those who do not have cars, riding buses can be just as good. To avoid distressing delays or disruptive events, be sure you have the exact fare. Apart from that, a bus ride can be entertaining for both caregiver and the person with Alzheimer's It allows a time of normalcy and contact with other passengers that can be enjoyable for everyone concerned.

Exercise

Exercise is vitally important and too often neglected. Lack of exercise may be one of the biggest factors in wandering in a number of cases. All older people need a good amount of exercise. It is said to be one of the biggest factors in "good" or "bad" aging, and this is still true in Alzheimer's. Since the disease eventually may manifest physical impairment, it is good to encourage the person with Alzheimer's to keep walking and exercising as much as possible. Caregivers report various experiences in their search for successful ways of exercising. Some have had success using television or video aerobics, but for many people the pace and the music is distressing.

Yoga and tai chi are both possible since they are slow and can be paced for older impaired people. Others can join in senior exercise classes in senior centers. Persons with Alzheimer's are usually welcome at any senior center as long as their caregiver accompanies them and takes responsibility for them.

Fingerwork

All those small, fidgety tasks that might happily occupy the person with Alzheimer's, come within the range of possible activities that are useful and produce a better sense of self-esteem. Many of them relate to normal life and can be regarded as variations of household tasks. They could include the following:
- cutting out coupons;
- cutting up greeting cards;

- chopping vegetables;
- folding sheets, towels, and pillowcases;
- winding balls of yarn;
- sorting things – but not necessarily successful if cognitive processing is needed, for example sorting quarters from dimes;
- taking things out of drawers;
- polishing shoes or cutlery.

All of the above, and whatever else you think of, can be deliberately used to engage the attention of someone with Alzheimer's. If you have never tried some of these things, you'll be surprised at how effectively they can occupy a person with dementia.

They are all useful to a certain extent in themselves and this makes an otherwise unoccupied person feel better. Having nothing to do all day and feeling useless make Alzheimer's even more of a prison.

Carrying out small helpful tasks lightens that sense of personal worthlessness common to nearly everyone with Alzheimer's. The tasks have the additional attraction of being occupational therapy, and this is why it can be useful for the caregiver to artificially extend the task. Thus, one family caregiver would deliberately carry the towels her mother had folded out of the room, then bring them back in disarray and ask her to fold them again.

She said, "I'd happily do it all afternoon as long as she felt useful and kept out of my hair!"

Games
Familiar games may still be possible for the person with Alzheimer's. You may have to remind people of games once enjoyed, since they may forget they know them.

You may also introduce new games that are easy to play. Take a look around a good toy store and see what games they have for younger children. A number of these may come within the range of possibility without insulting a person's sense of esteem. There are, for example, many games that involve putting things together or taking them apart. Jenga is a good game of this type. It is easy yet also absorbing, and everyone enjoys the blocks crashing down.

Building blocks can be fun, as can matching picture games. The visual often works where the verbal does not, so look for games that depend upon the visual and tactile senses.

You can create games by cutting out a number of pictures of people and asking the person to make up stories about them. Even a verbally impaired person can still make up a good story. One caregiver cut out reproductions of famous works of art, pasted them in an exercise book, and she and a woman with Alzheimer's told stories about them. Whistler's "Portrait of the Artist's Mother" was described as "being worried about something bad, I don't know what, but something anyway!"

Gardening

People who always loved to garden still get a great deal of comfort out of the emotionally familiar feeling of being out in the garden. Unfortunately, they may no longer be as skilled as they used to be, but it is worth trying to encourage them in their work as much as possible.

You might need to actually set them to work, to remind them of the tasks they used to do. Take them out to the garden, put a familiar tool in their hands, and show them what to do. Keep them to the simpler tasks such as weeding, trimming, or raking.

Be prepared for mistakes and just let them be, without reproaches. Maybe you will lose a few seedlings mistaken for weeds, but meanwhile you will have given a great gift to the person, the chance to be normal again doing something comfortable. If you think your charge might eat the plants, be sure to use only edible ones like pansies, marigolds, and petunias.

You can also do indoor gardening, planting bulbs in containers, using a protective covering over the kitchen table as you do this.

Housework

"Come on, Jane, come in and help us," called the respite center worker. Jane peered into the kitchen suspiciously.

"Come on what?" she demanded.

"Come on and help me with the washing up."

"No way, Jose!" said Jane. "I'm never going in one of those places again. I've done all that stuff I'm going to."

It was true, too. At home, Jane no longer cooked, washed dishes, or even went into the kitchen. Her husband thought it was because of her Alzheimer's disease, but the respite center staff wondered.

For those who do want to continue their familiar household tasks, there are many ways to help around the house even when profoundly afflicted with Alzheimer's. A wise caregiver will utilize any such abilities, not because they necessarily make the caregiver's task easier in an obvious sense—in fact, the helping may need supervision from the caregiver. However, it helps the impaired person to feel more useful and therefore improves general well-being.

Caregivers do well to lower their standards, if necessary, in order to let people with Alzheimer's help around the house. The kinds of useful things persons with Alzheimer's can do well are non-linear tasks, such as:
• folding laundry;
• wiping kitchen surfaces;
• washing up (although this probably won't be well done);

216

- preparing simple foods (to be done under supervision);
- making beds;
- cleaning windows;
- washing floors.

Of course, if all people with Alzheimer's could do all these things well, every family would want one living with them. In fact, abilities vary and so will the concentration span of each person. Hannah would carefully sweep all the dust into one neat pile and then, with a dramatic flourish of her brush, would scatter it back all over the room, saying, "There, that is good!"

Various tasks may not be completed and others will be done poorly. Linear, step-by-step tasks may fail completely. Laying a table correctly, for example, is a linear task involving learned behavior and logical thinking, both impaired in the person with Alzheimer's. The failure to lay a table properly often exasperates caregivers, who feel the person is being deliberately unhelpful, but it is a complex thinking task.

Encourage these people to help around the house as much as possible: to carry in the groceries with you, for example; to hold open a garbage bag while you put things in it; to brush the cat; to water a plant; to pile up newspapers. If they fail in their task, do not try to train them. A person with Alzheimer's cannot be trained to develop new habits. Just let it go.

Unfortunately, it is unlikely that major help with the housework will be forthcoming, but try to be grateful for small acts meant to help you. Anything that can help an impaired person to feel more useful is a great gift to that person. The worst thing you can do is say, "Don't worry, I can take of it," and keep the person useless.

Hugging

This is an extremely important activity and should be indulged in often. It is a wonderful form of communication when other kinds fail. It is effortless, rewarding, and happily addictive. When sitting with your arm around someone who has Alzheimer's, let go of your feeling that it is the other person who needs the hug and allow yourself to relax into the warm feeling of being close to another person.

Let go of your responsibilities and enjoy the human contact. Drink in the basic human touch and forget to be a caregiver for a little while. Then, you too will experience that we do not give out hugs, we share them, and loving energy is exchanged.

Music

Love of music remains whole even in the deeply afflicted. Singers still sing, musicians often still play if their instrument is actually put in their hands or their hands are put on the instrument. Those who loved to listen to music will still do so. Most people remember clearly the music of childhood and early adulthood and it usually has happy associations.

A caregiver can always get some rest by putting on a familiar piece of music and sitting down to relax with the person with Alzheimer's while both listen. Search out appropriate music on the radio, or get some CDs so you can instantly play something the person would enjoy. Music soothes bad moods and extends good ones and allows for undemanding companionship. It is relaxing to sit comfortably with your arm around the person as you both enjoy music together.

Pets

The cat arrived out of nowhere, a red stumpy-tailed tomcat with a torn-off ear. Hannah had never had a pet before her Alzheimer's disease, but she and Ginger—as the caregivers named him—hit it off immediately. Together they sat out in the sunshine by the bamboos and Hannah stroked him, saying, "Oh, you are such a beautiful little boy—no, not a little boy—a, well, you are—well, never mind, you are beautiful."

She never remembered what kind of animal Ginger was, but she knew their relationship was deeply enjoyable to her.

Pets can be especially rewarding for those with Alzheimer's. They are affectionate, nonverbal, and fun to touch. They have no awareness that their owner has Alzheimer's disease and therefore do not behave differently toward them. If you are a caregiver to someone who has never had a pet before, consider whether getting one might introduce a healthy new interest.

Even if someone has never had a pet or expressed liking animals before, pet companionship can be very successful for the person with Alzheimer's. A pet calls on the person's protectiveness and therefore creates a sense of power and wholeness. For the person who is largely home bound, a pet can provide new interest and entertainment.

If you decide to bring a new pet into the life of someone who has Alzheimer's, it is probably best to bring in an older animal who had previously to an elder. One of these can be ideal. They are already aged, used to elders, and well-socialized. It has been well documented that pets help the emotional and even physical health of many adults. They can do much to alleviate the loneliness and stress of having Alzheimer's disease.

If you decide to try this, be aware that you will have to care for the animal, but it might ease the burden of looking after the person with Alzheimer's. Make sure to take that person with you to choose the animal, so that a bond can exist from the beginning. Listen to what the person wants and honor those wishes, if possible.

Photographs

Most people like to look at photographs from time to time. People with Alzheimer's often appreciate having their memories reawakened by seeing pictures of family members. Even quite profoundly afflicted people can turn out to have a good recall of distant times, and looking through an album can be a pleasant way of passing an hour together. When married people look through pictures together, it helps them to recall times they spent happily together.

Contrary to what you might think, few people are depressed by such pictures. They do not, on the whole, make contrasts between their situation, then and now. They simply enjoy remembering that they had fun or went somewhere interesting. If no such albums exist, you might think about making one. You can write reminders under each picture. If you are a caregiver who comes from outside the family, it might be necessary to ask for some family cooperation to get relevant information, but it can really be worth the effort. Be sure to involve the person in the activity of choosing the pictures and putting them in an album.

Looking at photographs allows a quiet sharing and occupies the time. Remember that memory varies from day to day in someone who has Alzheimer's, so one day might open up a whole store of stories while another draws a blank. In Alzheimer's, more distant memories are often clearer, so the person's children may be recognized while more recent grandchildren may or may not be remembered easily.

Family members should try not to take this personally, since it is only a reflection of the way in that the memory is constructed and the way in that Alzheimer's destroys it.

Many older people enjoy talking about their own parents and their own young life, and this is equally true for those with Alzheimer's. Give them the chance whenever possible and encourage them in their stories. It is good for them to recall the times when they were fully functioning and could do many more things. Remember to respond positively. If you have heard the stories too many times, get someone else to sit and look through the pictures with them.

Shopping

The success of this activity varies. Some people become so distracted by the variety of goods available that the experience is distressing.

Martha cannot see well and she has Alzheimer's disease, so she cannot remember the names of the items she wants nor can she see what they look like. However, she still likes to go shopping, which she largely does by feel and intuition. Her intuition is almost always wrong, and her feeling memory is no better than her cognitive memory.

Her caregiver does not enjoy shopping with Martha, but Martha enjoys it, so they continue to shop together for small items. Martha's daughter does the major shopping, without Martha. Even those who dislike shopping usually love to go into a coffee shop or an ice cream parlor to eat something sweet. Take a window seat so that you can watch people strolling by. It gives you more possibilities for conversation.

Sight-Seeing

Brief visits or day trips can be successful and enjoyable for both caregiver and the person with Alzheimer's. However constricted life and understanding may become, many persons with Alzheimer's take great pleasure in stress-free outings. These may include such things as a walk in a park or garden, a drive to a nearby scenic spot, watching children playing in a nursery school, or looking in a pet shop window.

Hannah loves the zoo. She goes once a month, although she always says, "Oh, it has been so many years," every time she gets there. She likes the larger animals, although she does not know their names any more. She especially likes the camels. "They are so—so—gracious," she says.

Since many of the things enjoyed in the past may no longer be enjoyable because of changes in abilities and perceptions, it is worthwhile to try new things. Experimentation is always worthwhile, since boredom is often as great a part of caregiving as it is of having Alzheimer's disease. Include rides on buses, boats, and trains, if they can be stress-free.

Try picnics in the park, feeding the birds and squirrels, sitting on a bench in the sun, standing outside a nursery school watching children play. If visiting a museum or gallery, keep it short—perhaps half an hour, with a coffee break. Since caregivers are so often frantic, these outings can also serve to slow them down and bring a little calmness into their lives. The more that the caregiver and the person with Alzheimer's can enjoy together, the more the tension and hardship will decrease.

Therefore, finding new ways to pass the time is not an idle luxury, it is a psychic lifesaver.

Social Life

If people still enjoy the company of visitors, or have become more sociable in the course of their illness—people with Alzheimer's often lose the inhibitions that kept them reclusive before—encourage this.

Encourage family members or friends to drop by, and be prepared to suggest ways in which they could pass time with the person with Alzheimer's. Often the main reason that friends and family members do not visit is that they have not been educated in relating to the person who is impaired. If the caregiver suggests something definite for them to do, it helps the visitor to adjust and gives the person with Alzheimer's a realistic focus for the visit.

CHAPTER ELEVEN

"HELP, I'M GOING CRAZY!"
CARING FOR THE CAREGIVER

Looking after a person who has Alzheimer's disease is exceptionally demanding. The dementias are more demanding than obviously physical illnesses like cancer. Because people with Alzheimer's can look surprisingly well and fit, we are often deceived by this appearance. Because they look fine, caregivers tend to subconsciously make the assumption that they are fine— despite all the evidence to the contrary.

Then the caregivers wonder why they cannot cope with the demands of caring for someone who appears well. If the person with Alzheimer's looked as ill as the person in a comparable stage of cancer, we would clearly see how advanced the illness was. Someone with terminal cancer tends to look thin, often yellowish or livid white, and may be largely bedridden. Visible warnings remind us daily how ill the person is, and that reminder tempers our behavior and understanding.

However, a person with middle- or late-stage Alzheimer's may look well. This often deceives caregivers into blaming themselves for not being better at looking after this person. The person may appear cheerful, physically in good condition, able to walk about freely, full of energy. it is hard to remember how ill this person really is. It is even more difficult when outsiders reinforce this.

"Fred looks so good, doesn't he? It's hard to believe he's as bad as you say."

"I talked to Mom on the phone the other day and she sounded great. Just like old times. Are you sure she's got Alzheimer's?"

Friends and relatives mean no malice by remarks like this, but they make caregivers inwardly reproach themselves even more for their failures. It is more useful to compare the average family caregiver with the hired professional. If you wanted a registered nurse to look after your severely-impaired mother, for a start you would be forced to hire a nurse for each of three eight-hour shifts. This alone tells you how much attention the person with Alzheimer's needs.

As any family caregiver knows, looking after someone with Alzheimer's is a 24-hour task. Constant supervision, day and night, is essential. Unbroken sleep may be impossible. As well as taking over all the normal personal care and household chores, you may also have to help that person with every task of daily life, including dressing, washing, and going to the bathroom. As if that were not enough, you may have to keep explaining the world to the person, filling the sense gaps that are missing, soothing and calming. You may well have to repeat your answers and you may be unable to rely on that person's remembering one answer you gave.

Instead, you might be fully employed as a 24-hour interpreter, ready at any time day or night to make the connections your person cannot. Who on earth could do all that? The answer, unfortunately, is that the average family caregiver drives himself or herself to try. That is why the Alzheimer's Association reports that over 66 percent of home caregivers suffer from emotional and physical exhaustion due to the stress of caregiving. When elderly spouses are concerned, it is not uncommon for the well spouses to work themselves into the grave while their partners with Alzheimer's are still going strong.

STOP!

Stop now and take a hard look at what you do. Make a list of your daily tasks—all of them—from the practical assistance to the number of hours you have to remain constantly alert. Count the uninterrupted hours of sleep you get.

Make another list of the things you worry about. Add any concerns you have about your own health.

Now make a separate list of all the things you do to look after yourself. If that particular list is empty—and unfortunately it may well be—it is time to reevaluate.

You cannot go on endlessly coping alone. The price of doing that includes heart attacks, strokes, ulcers, and other catastrophic illnesses—and that is the good news. That assumes you will survive at all. Many people do not. They try so hard to look after someone—for example, a spouse—that they die and leave their spouse alone.

Alzheimer's cannot be coped with alone. It is self-destructive even to try It makes no sense. Like many people, you may have been brought up to believe that, whatever your troubles were, you dealt with them yourself. You did not ask others for help.

WRONG!

You must reach out to others for help. You have to get involved beyond your family if you are to get the support you need in order to survive the stress of caregiving. You have to become willing to ask for what you need instead of being private and concealing.

"I was ashamed of Claire when she got Alzheimer's. I got mad at her because she did strange things. If she did them in public, I felt like hitting her. She had a daughter but she never helped me with her mother. It was just me, and I'm afraid I wasn't very patient," says Virgil, whose wife Claire is now in a care home, after he was hospitalized with a stroke.

Perhaps you think you are not stressed, that you are managing well. Check out the following checklist from the Alzheimer's Association:

** Do you feel like you have to do it all yourself and that you should be doing more?

** Have you withdrawn from family, friends and activities that you used to enjoy?

** Do you worry if the person you care for is safe?

** Do you feel anxious about money and healthcare decisions?

** Do you deny the impact of the disease and its effects on your family?

** Do you feel grief or sadness that your relationship with the person isn't what it used to be?

** Do you get frustrated and angry when the person with dementia continually repeats things and doesn't seem to listen?

** Do you have health problems that are taking a toll on you mentally and physically?

If most of your answers are "Yes!" go and read more at

www.alz.org/care/alzheimers-dementia-stress-check.asp#ixzz24gN9GphT

We human beings manifest distress in hundreds of different ways. However, if you can tick off several of the items on the list, then believe it: You are suffering from stress. And stress kills. One of the best ways for you to begin dealing with the stress of being a caregiver is to make contact with other caregivers.

"It took me far too long to join a support group," says Jean. "I should have joined as soon as I started taking care of my mother, but I said to myself, 'I'm a nurse. I know how to take care of people. It's my profession.' But it's different when it's your own mother or spouse. You need to be able to talk things over with other people who really know what it's like."

Many families seek the help of support groups because they feel abandoned in their struggle with Alzheimer's. It is not, as you might fear, just a bunch of people complaining to each other. It is a group of people who sometimes complain—certainly—but who give each other good information, have a whole range of suggestions for coping with problems, who represent among them selves a wide range of experience, knowledge, and ideas for deal in with Alzheimer's.

Support group members have access to the experience of Alzheimer's in a way that no medical professional, no social worker—no one who does not actually live with the disease—can share. They can recommend a good doctor, a particularly helpful social worker, or a great day-care program. They can also ease your burden simply by knowing how you feel without your having to explain.

"I got Edie up three times yesterday, got her dressed, and each time when I came back, she was back under the covers undressed again. I could have killed her," says Wayne. The group nods feelingly. They have all known those moments of frustration. "Sometimes I fantasize about putting her out on the freeway just when an eighteen-wheeler is coming along."

The group laughs, because they understand exactly how Wayne feels and they know he is only partly joking. When he gets home, Wayne feels better just because he has not been alone and because he could tell these people his secrets and not be condemned by them.

Find a support group through the Alzheimer's Association web page. Also check your local newspaper or ask at the public library. reference desk. Most Alzheimer's support groups in this country are sponsored by the national Alzheimer's Association, which does the supremely helpful task of putting out information and newsletters, as well as organizing training and workshops, in addition to national advocacy and fund-raising for research into the cause, treatment, and cure of Alzheimer's disease.

All Alzheimer's Association groups are free of charge. Their facilitators are unpaid volunteers who are usually highly knowledgeable about living with Alzheimer's disease.

You may also find other free local support groups, perhaps organized through your local hospital as a community service or as part of a local day-respite program. Some groups might be for all home caregivers, not Alzheimer specific. If this is all that is available, you would probably find it useful. Most Alzheimer and dementia caregivers find specific groups more helpful, but all full-time caregiving is equally troublesome and therefore all caregivers can help each other.

However overstressed you are right now, you can immediately begin to change the way in which you are living your life.

The first step in doing this is to recognize that you have a supreme responsibility to take care of yourself first. Without that, you cannot be a good caregiver. If you do not take steps to deal with your stress, then your stress will deal with you. It may feel selfish or just plain impossible, or you may not know how to put yourself first. After all, you still have that other person totally needing your care. How could you possibly put yourself first?

This is the center of the Alzheimer caregiver's real problem. It is not that caregiving in itself has to be so stressful. It is that disregarding one's own needs causes huge stress.

"I kept telling myself I could take time for me when Sam was dead. But it's been five years now and this year the doctor said my stomach pains were due to an ulcer. He said if I didn't stop, Sam would outlive me anyway," Rachel says.

Her doctor recommended medication for her ulcer and a therapist for her stress. "The therapist helped me to see that all my problems were not due to Sam's Alzheimer's, but partly to do with how I coped. I kept thinking I couldn't possibly feel better until his Alzheimer's was solved. She helped me see I could feel better right now if I dealt with my stress."

Rachel has not changed her routine radically, but she has made changes that help her refocus. She takes soothing baths with healing oils. She goes to a movie once a week by herself. She gets up earlier so she can have an hour of peace in the morning before Sam awakes.

"Sam's as ill as ever but I'm doing better," she says.

And you too can do better by acknowledging that you do need help from outside and planning your campaign for obtaining it. Getting assistance also means asking family members to give practical help and being very specific about what, when, why, and how they will help. Often, family members resist vaguer suggestions because you allow them space to evade your request.

"I wish you would help more" is likely to bring the answer, "Oh yes, well, I'll try," and no actual practical contribution. It is harder for a family member to evade when you say, "I want to go to that painting class I told you about. Will you come on Wednesday evenings and sit with your father, please?"

The same is true with friends and neighbors. Unfortunately, you cannot always count on your friends to be around when Alzheimer's strikes. Joanne's story is typical.

"Our friends just slowly disappeared when Harold got Alzheimer's," she recalls. "These weren't casual friends. They were two or three couples we had known for years— gone on holiday with them, spent Thanksgiving and Christmas with them. Gradually they were no longer around and we stopped getting invitations. I can't tell you how much that hurt me. The sorrow is even greater than the loneliness I feel. How could they do that to us?"

We all know that some friends are better than others in times of trouble. In fact, some people are actually better friends when we are in trouble than when life is going smoothly. People have different coping skills, and the nearer a problem gets to their own fear level, the further away some people are likely to be—unless they are emotionally mature people. Being older, alas, is no guarantee of emotional maturity. Alzheimer's strikes at the very heart of most people's fear. center.

Those who dread Alzheimer's fear that it means loss, dependency on others, lack of freedom, perhaps lack of dignity, not being able to count on oneself any more. The older people get, the more they fear this disease they hear so much about. When someone they know and love, someone who has been as competent as themselves, is diagnosed as having it, many people run.

On the other hand, not everyone behaves like this. When Mike found that his wife had Alzheimer's, he called together twelve of their closest friends for a meeting. "Mabel has Alzheimer's disease,"he began. "I know you'll all be sorry to hear that and I know it might make some of you want to avoid us. I'll understand if you do that, but I sure will miss you and so will Mabel."

That gave his friends an unusual opportunity to discuss their own feelings and fears about Alzheimer's. After a while, Mike continued: "Now here's what we're going to need. I have to stay up nights pretty often now since Mabel gets up and wanders about. So if any of you could come over in the mornings sometimes, so I could catch up a bit on my sleep, why, that'd be just dandy. And you know I still like to fish, so if any of you ladies would take Mabel out for coffee or home for lunch so I can get a break that way, well, that'd be just great too."

He told his friends what he needed and how much he and Mabel still wanted their friends' love and help and company. At last report, Mike said they'd only lost one couple from their social group. The others were chipping in with help and relief whenever they could and they still invited Mike and Mabel over, accepting that Mike could not return their hospitality the same way.

That is a rare success story but probably not because such friends are rare. More likely, the rarity was Mike's courage and honesty in putting out his needs and the risk he took in really reaching out to his friends. Not many people are as brave as Mike.

It is much more usual for people to say, "There's no help out there," rather than learn how to ask for it in the right way. It is probably part of the older generation's phony pride that says one must cope alone. It takes real courage to ask, and it is true there is no guarantee of success. One woman had been encouraged by her support group to ask a friend to take her mother out occasionally.

Later she reported back to the group: "I asked Mother's friend Sallie if she'd help me by taking Mother for a drive. She said she couldn't take responsibility for her!"

Do make sure your neighbors know about your family member's condition. That way, they will become part of your defense system. Often others hesitate only because they are not sure if they would be welcome in their intervention. Plus, they may fear they will hurt or upset the person with Alzheimer's if they do not always know exactly how to deal with him or her.

"I think our neighbor's husband has Alzheimer's. He has that kind of lost look about him," Phyllis says. "I've tried to make conversation with her, so I could offer some help, but she won't talk to me apart from saying hello."

Even the most loving caregiver thinks, sometimes sadly and sometimes longingly, of being released from a burden by the death of the person with Alzheimer's. It is true there will be problems and situations to be dealt with until death does occur. However, the stress of dealing with the situation can be alleviated at any moment by the actions we take.

The Chinese say: "If you can't change a situation, you must change your mind."

You can deal with stress right now by taking ten slow, deep breaths. And you can do this several times a day every day—especially before you sleep, when you get up, and during any particularly stressful time. You can do some basic stretching exercises to help your muscle tension. You can soak in a hot scented tub for a while. You can buy a bunch of flowers and look at them with enjoyment. You can write down a list of everything that is worrying you and cross off all items you cannot do anything about here and now.

You can stop fighting the fact of Alzheimer's and accept that it is here and it will have certain effects on the person who has it.

You can look into stress management classes at your local senior center or community college. You can learn how to deal with tension, headaches, and other bodily symptoms. You can take up meditation, self-hypnosis, yoga, tai chi, relaxation. Actually, you undoubtedly already know many of the ways you could instantly reduce your stress. It is limited only by your unwillingness to let go of your stress.

That may sound odd to you but, after all, only you can choose to deal with your stress. You can ease it, if you choose to do so, or you can elect to stay addicted to it. However, this habit burns out your system and brings about the physical and emotional collapse not unusual among Alzheimer caregivers. Ask yourself if you really want to let go of your stress. If your automatic reaction is "Yes, of course I do!" then ask yourself HOW you will let go of it. Look at your excuses. No time to breathe? No time to stretch? No time to take a bath? These are the excuses of someone addicted to stress.

It is not admirable to work yourself literally into the grave looking after someone else. We caregivers all need to deal with our own unhealthy patterns, not blame them on disease. So here are some excellent ways to change your stress level.

DO take your relative to day-care respite programs. He or she will probably enjoy it much more than you think. You are much too busy to provide the attention, fun, and activities that the program offers. Often people find it extremely comforting to be among others with the same level of ability.

DO join a support group. They really do work for people. Most people who join them felt exactly as you do right now. It is scary to go to strangers and be prepared to share your struggles with them.

DO admit that you are not a perfect caregiver. That allows you to admit your impatience and stops it being your secret burden. It allows you to allow someone else into your little universe of caregiving.

DO stop trying to fool yourself that you are indispensable. You are not the only person who can meet the needs of the relative you look after. Actually, others may do some of it better than you do.

DO take a long hard look at your real feelings. Perhaps you resent your loss of freedom, or the ruined life you feel you have now. Perhaps you even find yourself disliking your sick partner because of his or her constant needs. These are the usual feelings human beings get uncomfortable about when caught up in long-term stress situations.

As you begin dealing with your stress, you will find that you become much freer to cope with things. You will discover interesting new solutions to old problems.

You may well find an interesting new you that comes up with a whole new way to arrange life. If you make room in your life for yourself you will certainly find solutions that work for you.

RESOURCES

As well as the sites included here, consider the Mayo Clinic site as your basic information source. They are not tightly-linked to the drug industry and have a full and reasonable fact-based site on almost any health issue you could think of. You can just Google Mayo Clinic and whatever else you want to know about.

As an amateur who needs to know about medical issues, like most caregivers, I rate the Mayo Clinic site above any of the Federal Government sites, such as any of the National Institutes of Health. The difference is in tone and attitude and the Mayo Clinic is sharing useful medical information about diseases, current known facts in medical practice and reasonable commentary on treatments and approaches to illness conditions.

The NIH are less communicative, harder to navigate and often involved with drug company co-experimental developments.   They   are   essentially   government departments.

Keep checking your resources. Improvements and new approaches to dementia care are always being explored and one day one of those discoveries will be the one you are hoping for.

ALZHEIMER'S ASSOCIATION
National Headquarters
Alzheimer's Association National Office, 225 N. Michigan Ave., Fl. 17, Chicago, IL 60601
Alzheimer's Association is a not-for-profit 501(c)(3) organization.

The major national resource available for the families of those with Alzheimer's disease is the Alzheimer's Association. This non-profit organization raises funds for research into Alzheimer's disease and related dementias and offers informational support to caregivers, as well as offering free support groups for everyone dealing with Alzheimer's disease. These groups are available all over the country and there is sure to be one somewhere near you.

Find the Alzheimer's Association online at www.alz.org. That is the best site to start out your quest. You will get facts, connections, a country-wide network of support groups, conferences, phone numbers, on-line help and support. They have an 24/7 toll-free support
  Helpline: 1.800.272.3900.

ALZHEIMER'S FOUNDATION OF AMERICA
www.alzfdn.org

LEWY BODY DEMENTIA:
  Lewy Body Dementia Organization: online at www.lbda.org/
    www.mayoclinic.org/lewy-body-dementia/

FRONTOTEMPORAL DEMENTIA
  The Association for Frontotemporal Degeneration: online at www.theaftd.org/
    Frontotemporal Dementia Caregiver Support Center at ftdsupport.com

VASCULAR DEMENTIA
  Vascular dementia info from The National Stroke Association at   www.stroke.org
    www.mayoclinic.com/health/vascular-dementia/DS00934/

WERNICKE-KORSAKOFF DEMENTIA
  www.ncbi.nlm.nih.gov
  www.caregiver.org
  yowww.caspalmera.com/articles/wernicke-korsakoff-syndrome-and-how-it-can-affectyou

PARKINSON'S DISEASE

Parkinson's Disease Foundation: www.pdf.org. They have a good website and send you free information.

The Michael Fox Organization has a more lively and upbeat style with lots of info on any of the latest developments in Parkinson's treatments: www.michaeljfox.org:

Most of these organizations have online blogs and forums where you can learn more and chat with other caregivers.

Another good site for caregivers is www.caring.com. All kinds of caregivers are there, not just dementia caregivers. Plus it has many helpful articles. For dementia, I have found that this site is not discerning enough, when it comes to different dementias, nor careful enough about symptoms and what they mean. There is too much of an assumption that everything is Alzheimer's and a serious omission is the issue of mentally ill elders being wrongly diagnosed as people with Alzheimer's. However, it is overall friendly, useful and non-technical.

How to Contact Frena Gray-Davidson

My website is www.speakingdementia.com and you can always contact me through that site. I am usually prompt at replying to emails and enjoy receiving them. If you have ideas for improvement in this book, please share them with me.

My books are available on www.amazon.com in print and in Kindle. If you would like to place a wholesale order, for your organization, please email my publisher at Balian Books, email address balianbooks@gmail.com.

I am happy to do staff training, talks to caregivers and conference presentations both in the USA and Canada, as well as overseas. Please contact me through my website or via my publisher. I specially like to go to Asia and Polynesian islands, just so you know.

May all caregivers find peace and fulfillment on the noble path of caregiving.

Made in the USA
Lexington, KY
07 January 2013